Ancient
Mesopotamia

by
Don Nardo

LUCENT BOOKS

THOMSON

GALE

San Diego • Detroit • New York • San Francisco • Cleveland • New Haven, Conn. • Waterville, Maine • London • Munich

THOMSON

GALE

LIBRARY OF CONGRESS CATALOGING-IN-PUBLICATION DATA

Nardo, Don, 1947–.
    Ancient Mesopotamia / by Don Nardo.
        p. cm. — (World history series)
    Summary: A historical overview of the rise of the Assyrians and Babylonians and the culture
they developed in Ancient Mesopotamia, plus a glimpse of the region in later centuries.
Includes bibliographical references and index.
      ISBN 1-59018-292-8 (lib. bdg. : alk. paper)
      1. Iraq—Juvenile literature. [1. Iraq—Civilization—To 634.] I.
Title. II. Series.
    DS70.62.N37 2004
    935—dc22

                                                      2003012841

Printed in the United States of America

Contents

Foreword

Each year on the first day of school, nearly every history teacher faces the task of explaining why his or her students should study history. One logical answer to this question is that exploring what happened in our past explains how the things we often take for granted—our customs, ideas, and institutions—came to be. As statesman and historian Winston Churchill put it, "Every nation or group of nations has its own tale to tell. Knowledge of the trials and struggles is necessary to all who would comprehend the problems, perils, challenges, and opportunities which confront us today." Thus, a study of history puts modern ideas and institutions in perspective. For example, though the founders of the United States were talented and creative thinkers, they clearly did not invent the concept of democracy. Instead, they adapted some democratic ideas that had originated in ancient Greece and with which the Romans, the British, and others had experimented. An exploration of these cultures, then, reveals their very real connection to us through institutions that continue to shape our daily lives.

Another reason often given for studying history is the idea that lessons exist in the past from which contemporary societies can benefit and learn. This idea, although controversial, has always been an intriguing one for historians. Those who agree that society can benefit from the past often quote philosopher George Santayana's famous statement, "Those who cannot remember the past are condemned to repeat it." Historians who subscribe to Santayana's philosophy believe that, for example, studying the events that led up to the major world wars or other significant historical events would allow society to chart a different and more favorable course in the future.

Just as difficult as convincing students of the importance of studying history is the search for useful and interesting supplementary materials that present historical events in a context that can be easily understood. The volumes in Lucent Books' World History Series attempt to present a broad, balanced, and penetrating view of the march of history. Ancient Egypt's important wars and rulers, for example, are presented against the rich and colorful backdrop of Egyptian religious, social, and cultural developments. The series engages the reader by enhancing historical events with these cultural contexts. For example, in *Ancient Greece*, the text covers the role of women in that society. Slavery is discussed in *The Roman Empire*, as well as how slaves earned their freedom. The numerous and varied aspects of everyday life in these and other societies are explored in each volume of the series. Additionally, the series covers the major political, cultural, and philosophical ideas as the torch of civilization is passed from ancient Mesopotamia and Egypt, through Greece, Rome, Medieval Europe, and other world cultures, to the modern day.

The material in the series is formatted in a thorough, precise, and organized manner.

Each volume offers the reader a comprehensive and clearly written overview of an important historical event or period. The topic under discussion is placed in a broad, historical context. For example, *The Italian Renaissance* begins with a discussion of the High Middle Ages and the loss of central control that allowed certain Italian cities to develop artistically. The book ends by looking forward to the Reformation and interpreting the societal changes that grew out of the Renaissance. Thus, students are not only involved in an historical era, but also enveloped by the events leading up to that era and the events following it.

One important and unique feature in the World History Series is the primary and secondary source quotations that richly supplement each volume. These quotes are useful in a number of ways. First, they allow students access to sources they would not normally be exposed to because of the difficulty and obscurity of the original source. The quotations range from interesting anecdotes to farsighted cultural perspectives and are drawn from historical witnesses both past and present. Second, the quotes demonstrate how and where historians themselves derive their information on the past as they strive to reach a consensus on historical events. Lastly, all of the quotes are footnoted, familiarizing students with the citation process and allowing them to verify quotes and/or look up the original source if the quote piques their interest.

Finally, the books in the World History Series provide a detailed launching point for further research. Each book contains a bibliography specifically geared toward student research. A second, annotated bibliography introduces students to all the sources the author consulted when compiling the book. A chronology of important dates gives students an overview, at a glance, of the topic covered. Where applicable, a glossary of terms is included.

In short, the series is designed not only to acquaint readers with the basics of history, but also to make them aware that their lives are a part of an ongoing human saga. Perhaps then they will come to the same realization as famed historian Arnold Toynbee. In his monumental work, *A Study of History*, he wrote about becoming aware of history flowing through him in a mighty current, and of his own life "welling like a wave in the flow of this vast tide."

IMPORTANT DATES IN ANCIENT MESOPOTAMIA

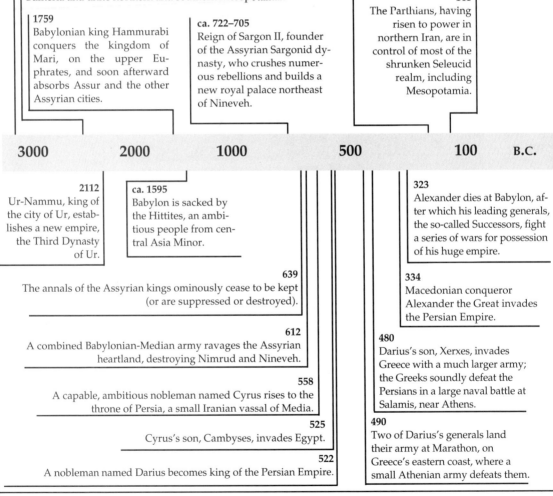

ca. 3300–3000
The Sumerians build the first Mesopotamian cities in the plain just northwest of the Persian Gulf; they also begin using a complex writing system that evolves into what modern scholars call cuneiform.

ca. 2400–2200
Akkadian rulers, most prominent among them King Sargon, conquer Sumeria and unite northern and southern Mesopotamia.

1759
Babylonian king Hammurabi conquers the kingdom of Mari, on the upper Euphrates, and soon afterward absorbs Assur and the other Assyrian cities.

ca. 722–705
Reign of Sargon II, founder of the Assyrian Sargonid dynasty, who crushes numerous rebellions and builds a new royal palace northeast of Nineveh.

281
After carving out a new Near Eastern empire centered in Mesopotamia, one of the Successors, Seleucus, dies.

141
The Parthians, having risen to power in northern Iran, are in control of most of the shrunken Seleucid realm, including Mesopotamia.

| 3000 | 2000 | 1000 | 500 | 100 | B.C. |

2112
Ur-Nammu, king of the city of Ur, establishes a new empire, the Third Dynasty of Ur.

ca. 1595
Babylon is sacked by the Hittites, an ambitious people from central Asia Minor.

639
The annals of the Assyrian kings ominously cease to be kept (or are suppressed or destroyed).

612
A combined Babylonian-Median army ravages the Assyrian heartland, destroying Nimrud and Nineveh.

558
A capable, ambitious nobleman named Cyrus rises to the throne of Persia, a small Iranian vassal of Media.

525
Cyrus's son, Cambyses, invades Egypt.

522
A nobleman named Darius becomes king of the Persian Empire.

323
Alexander dies at Babylon, after which his leading generals, the so-called Successors, fight a series of wars for possession of his huge empire.

334
Macedonian conqueror Alexander the Great invades the Persian Empire.

480
Darius's son, Xerxes, invades Greece with a much larger army; the Greeks soundly defeat the Persians in a large naval battle at Salamis, near Athens.

490
Two of Darius's generals land their army at Marathon, on Greece's eastern coast, where a small Athenian army defeats them.

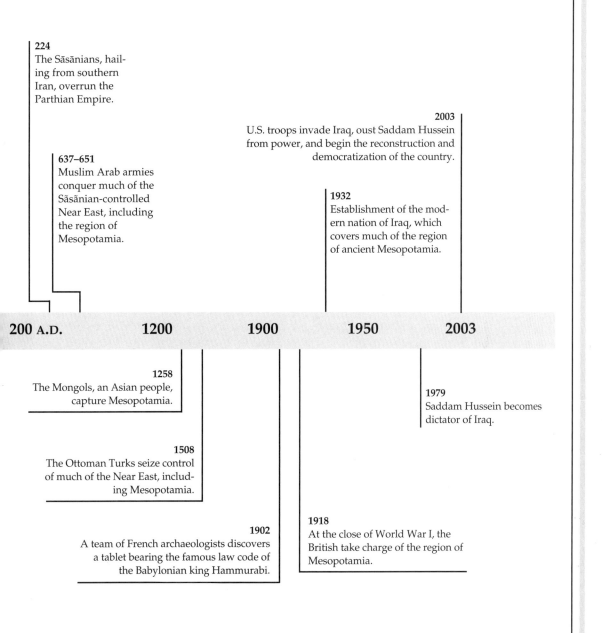

224
The Sāsānians, hailing from southern Iran, overrun the Parthian Empire.

637–651
Muslim Arab armies conquer much of the Sāsānian-controlled Near East, including the region of Mesopotamia.

2003
U.S. troops invade Iraq, oust Saddam Hussein from power, and begin the reconstruction and democratization of the country.

1932
Establishment of the modern nation of Iraq, which covers much of the region of ancient Mesopotamia.

200 A.D.   **1200**   **1900**   **1950**   **2003**

1258
The Mongols, an Asian people, capture Mesopotamia.

1979
Saddam Hussein becomes dictator of Iraq.

1508
The Ottoman Turks seize control of much of the Near East, including Mesopotamia.

1902
A team of French archaeologists discovers a tablet bearing the famous law code of the Babylonian king Hammurabi.

1918
At the close of World War I, the British take charge of the region of Mesopotamia.

Who Were the First Mesopotamians?

The term "Mesopotamia" means "the land between the rivers" and originally referred to the mostly flat plains lying between the Tigris and Euphrates Rivers, in what is now Iraq. In time, most of the plains and hills surrounding the rivers, together making up the central portion of the Near East, also came to be thought of as part of Mesopotamia. In addition, "Mesopotamian" became a general name for any and all of the peoples who either inhabited or ruled over that region in ancient times; thus, the Sumerians, Akkadians, Assyrians, Babylonians, Elamites, Medes, and Persians, among others, were all Mesopotamians.

Mesopotamia was not just central to the Near East in the geographical sense. It was the site of the world's first true cities and literate cultures as well. It was also a busy crossroads of trade routes running between Palestine, Egypt, and the eastern Mediterranean in the east, Asia Minor (now Turkey) and Armenia in the north, Arabia in the south, and Afghanistan and India in the west. In addition, Mesopotamia was the heartland of a series of nations and empires that controlled large sections of the Near East over the centuries.

HUMAN ADVANCES IN THE FERTILE CRESCENT

Historians and laymen alike have long wondered who first settled this crucial crossroads of cultures. Where did they come from and when did they initially arrive? Early modern scholars assumed that Mesopotamia was the first part of the Near East to be settled. More specifically, they thought that the so-called cradle of civilization was in Sumer (the homeland of the Sumerians), situated in Mesopotamia's southeastern quarter near the Persian Gulf. Eventually, however, it became clear that the Sumerians were not the first settlers in the area; also, even their predecessors migrated there from somewhere else, which means that the cradle of civilization was located outside of Mesopotamia.

In fact, the Near East's initial inhabited zone was the Fertile Crescent, a broad belt of foothills surrounding the Mesopotamian plains. The crescent ran from central Palestine northward through Syria and eastern Asia Minor, then turned eastward and encompassed northern Iraq and Iran. As early as 9000 B.C., this region witnessed the beginnings of agriculture and raising livestock. "The first step now appears to have been the taming of goats and sheep," noted historian Chester G. Starr writes.

[Then] came the deliberate cultivation of two kinds of wheat and barley with some vegetables, and the domestication of pigs and cattle. . . . Normally, [these early agriculturalists] dwelled in open villages. Their houses occasionally collapsed in violent storms and rains, but the inhabitants were so sedentary [tending to stay in one place] that they simply rebuilt their houses on top of the ruins.[1]

Over time, agriculture and herding provided more food, which in turn stimulated population growth. And the addition of more people naturally increased the size and complexity of human settlements. "The activities of farming and shepherding required an intensification of group organization," Starr points out. "A phenomenal increase in physical possessions resulted from the needs of more developed life, much greater population, and more sedentary routines."[2]

By the eighth millennium B.C. (the 7000s B.C.), therefore, some of the original villages in the Fertile Crescent had grown larger and more sophisticated. The most

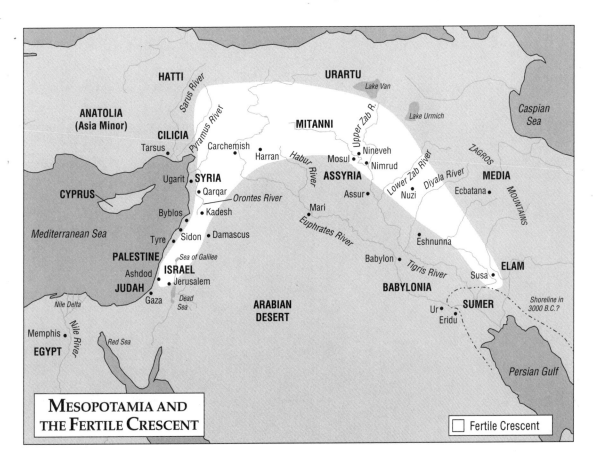

MESOPOTAMIA AND THE FERTILE CRESCENT

☐ Fertile Crescent

advanced of all began to protect themselves with defensive walls of brick and stone. Perhaps the best known of these early walled towns was Jericho, in the Jordan valley in Palestine, featuring stone defenses enclosing an area of eleven acres.

Larger still (at about thirty-two acres) was Çatal Hüyük, which flourished in southeastern Asia Minor in the seventh and sixth millennia B.C. This settlement, writes prolific historian Michael Grant,

> presents what may be the earliest known example of houses that are formally planned and grouped. Rectangular in shape . . . these buildings for the first time [in history] look something like a town. Urbanization is coming into existence. . . . Such an

urban concentration . . . leads to interchanges of ideas, techniques, forms of organization, and artistic styles.[3]

SOUTHWARD MIGRATIONS

Eventually, some of the inhabitants of the villages and small fortified towns of the Fertile Crescent began moving southward onto the plains of Mesopotamia. Almost all modern experts agree that this important turning point occurred sometime between 6000 and 5500 B.C. The exact reasons for the migrations are unclear. One possibility is excess population growth in the hills, causing some families, clans, or other groups to seek new homesteads in less crowded areas. One of the greatest scholars of Mesopotamian civilization, Samuel N. Kramer, suggests another reason; namely,

An aerial view of excavations at Çatal Hüyük, in southeastern Asia Minor. Many of the close-packed, rectangular houses shared their walls.

the migrations were caused by social and/or political frictions and discontent among some groups in the Fertile Crescent:

> As ironic fate would have it, the progress and unprecedented prosperity that the economic revolution [of agriculture] had brought to the proliferating [multiplying] northern villages also brought in its wake new groups of the depressed and oppressed, the disgruntled and dissatisfied. These malcontents had nothing to lose and everything to gain by breaking away from their neighbors and emigrating to the southern marshlands of Mesopotamia.[4]

Still another possibility is that a huge natural catastrophe set these migrations in motion. This theory, recently proposed by a group of scholars that includes Columbia University scientists William Ryan and Walter Pitman, suggests that the Fertile Crescent initially included the region of the Black Sea. They point to evidence showing that before the sixth millennium B.C. part of it was dry land and part a shallow freshwater lake. Today the Black Sea is connected to the Aegean and Mediterranean Seas by two straits—the Bosporus and Dardanelles. Originally, however,

French artist Gustav Dore's 1866 engraving of the biblical flood.

say Ryan and Pitman, the Bosporus was blocked by a huge earthen dam and the lake's level was hundreds of feet lower than that of the seas beyond.

The catastrophe came in about 5600 B.C. The Bosporus dam burst and enormous amounts of salt water rushed into the Black Sea lake, flooding its shores for many miles inland. Because the date of this disaster roughly coincides with that of the initial movement of peoples southward into Mesopotamia, supporters of the theory contend that these migrations were caused by large numbers of refugees fleeing their lakeside villages and farms. (They also speculate that the memory of the disaster gave rise to the legends of the great flood mentioned in several ancient Near Eastern texts, including the Old Testament.) According to Ryan and Pitman, ten cubic miles of water poured through the gap in the dam each day, "two-hundred times what flows over Niagara Falls, enough to cover Manhattan Island each day to a depth of over half a mile." Speculating on the human toll, they write:

> It is hard to imagine the terror of those farmers, forced from their fields by an event they could not understand, a force of such incredible violence that it was as if the collected fury of all the gods was being hurled at them. They fled with family, the old and the young, carrying what they could. . . . The speakers of the Semitic tongues climbed through the hills to the south. . . . A few of these . . . ventured to the middle of the southern Mesopotamian alluvium [river plain]. . . . These people, who knew how to irrigate, and may even have used a light plow, flourished.[5]

A FERTILE REGION

Whatever the motivations for the migrations, those early Mesopotamian pioneers who did have knowledge of irrigation held a decided advantage over those who did not. This was because the area was generally more arid than the hills, and to be successful the immigrants had to find effective ways to water their crops. Still, the Mesopotamian plains were not nearly as arid as they are today. Large areas were fertile and amenable to farming. And extensive marshes existed in many places along the riverbanks and near the Persian Gulf, which was a good deal larger in those days. "At the height of the last Ice Age, ca. 15,000 B.C.," noted scholar H.W.F. Saggs explains,

> the Persian Gulf was dry land. As the earth warmed up and the ice caps melted, sea level rose, until by 5000 B.C. or soon after, the Persian Gulf stood up to 9 feet above its present level. The head of the Gulf was then 100 miles or so northwest of its present position, and south Mesopotamia was less arid than much of it is today.[6]

As new bands of people from the Fertile Crescent and other areas made their way into Mesopotamia over the ensuing centuries, a network of lush fields and prosperous villages slowly grew along the riverbanks. Still more centuries passed. And some of the villages steadily became larger and more organized. In this way, the stage was set for the emergence of kings, city-states, empires, armies, and writing, signaling the beginning of Mesopotamia's long and turbulent recorded history.

1 The First Cities, Empires, and Literature

Between about 6000 and 3000 B.C., immigrants from the hilly regions lying west, north, and east of what is now Iraq settled on the plains of the Tigris and Euphrates River valleys, the area that became known as Mesopotamia. The most successful of these early groups were the Sumerians. From a modern viewpoint, they are the first important and certainly the most culturally influential Mesopotamians. All later peoples who inhabited the region in ancient times preserved or copied numerous aspects of Sumerian political and social customs, literature, and artistic styles.

The Sumerians had settled in the flatlands of southeastern Mesopotamia, just northwest of the Persian Gulf, by about 3100 B.C. (The word "Sumer" comes from the later Babylonian name for this region. The Sumerians themselves called the area Kengir, meaning "civilized land.") They probably gained control of the region by conquering the less-organized farmers and hunters who lived there already. Modern scholars call that earlier, more primitive culture Ubaidian, after al-Ubaid, the place where its remains were first discovered.

Once in control of southern Mesopotamia, the Sumerians developed writing, which allowed their rulers and nobles to record their myths, economic transactions, and political decrees. This significantly increased the effectiveness of their organization and authority. At the same time, they rapidly began building the first cities. As Yale University scholar Karen R. Nemet-Nejat puts it, they "turned an agricultural community into the first urban civilization in the world."[7] Several factors made these towns different from any that had come before. On the one hand, they were much larger. Typical was Lagash, on the southern bank of the Tigris, which had a population of some thirty-six thousand people and covered an area of more than two square miles. Also, such cities were built primarily of sun-dried or baked mud bricks and featured sturdy outer defensive walls.

Even more distinctive and revolutionary was the fact that these cities were not simply large, populous towns but also true city-states, each the central focus of a political unit that controlled a large expanse of farmland and supporting villages. Thus, they were not dependent units within a larger Sumerian nation but tiny independent nations in their own right. There was bound to be competition among these states. And this in turn led to war and the rise of even larger political

UBAIDIAN INFLUENCE ON THE SUMERIANS

In this excerpt from her recent book *Daily Life in Ancient Mesopotamia,* Yale University scholar Karen R. Nemet-Nejat gives this useful thumbnail sketch of the cultural influence the Ubaidians had on the Sumerians, who took over the area in which the Ubaidians dwelled and steadily absorbed the native population.

"The Ubaidians established a number of agricultural villages and towns throughout Mesopotamia. Archaeological finds attest to their development of skilled crafts; the Ubaidians left behind hoes, axes, knives, sickles, bricks, spindle whorls [for making thread], loom weights, sculpture, and painted pottery. Temples, enlarged over time, have been found at their sites. The Sumerians borrowed from them the names for occupations such as farmer, herdsman, fisherman, potter, carpenter, metalworker, leather worker, mason, weaver, basket maker, merchant, and priest. Other non-Sumerian words [that the Sumerians borrowed from the Ubaidians] include those for plow, furrow, palm, and date. Clearly, the development of these skills can be credited to these early settlers."

units—in effect the world's first empires. "Competition between cities . . . became intense," writes scholar Gwendolyn Leick,

and there was at times an aggressive expansionism at the expense of weaker rivals, fanned by political leaders whose power was based on military success and control over agricultural resources. According to the surviving written records, each ruler vaunted himself as a rightful leader by virtue of divine favor—as one chosen by the gods.[8]

It was only a matter of time before one such leader became powerful enough to conquer many cities and rule them as an empire. As it turned out, this early imperialist, Sargon, was not Sumerian but Akkadian, the general name of the peoples living in central Mesopotamia at the time.

It is essential to realize that the Akkadians were not racially, ethnically, or socially different from their southern neighbors, the Sumerians. In fact, both peoples, along with the Babylonians, Assyrians, and other Mesopotamian peoples who succeeded them, were all part of one big racial, ethnic, and cultural melting pot. The only significant differences were language and feelings of loyalty to one's local region or tribal roots. About this melting pot, H.W.F. Saggs says: "The cultural pressure of

Mesopotamian society ensured that although many diverse ethnic groups entered Mesopotamia, all were eventually assimilated, and none permanently stood apart."[9]

THE EARLY SUMERIAN CITY-STATES

The story of how the Sumerians and Akkadians vied for control of Mesopotamia's great melting pot of cities and peoples begins with the rise of the very first Sumerian city. Exactly which one actually appeared first is still debated by scholars. Among the leading candidates is Uruk, situated on the banks of the Euphrates about 160 miles northwest of the Persian Gulf. (In the Old Testament, the city is called Erech.) Uruk was already a fair-sized town by 4000 B.C. In the centuries that followed, the first known monumental (large-scale) stone buildings were erected there. (Their decayed and eroded remains still rise as high as fifty

The excavated remains of a religious temple at Uruk (the biblical Erech). No one knows when the city was founded, but it was flourishing by 4000 B.C.

feet.) And shortly after 3000 B.C., Uruk underwent a major burst of expansion in which tens of thousands of people moved in and a six-mile-long defensive wall was erected around the city. After visiting the present-day ruins of this ancient metropolis, historian Michael Wood wrote:

> The center of the city is dominated by the ruins of a great stepped tower, a ziggurat on which once stood a temple of the city's goddess, Inanna, whom we know as Ishtar. [The Greeks identified her with Aphrodite, goddess of love.] The first city may have begun as a religious center, perhaps a shrine for the herders of the plain. . . . The goddess's sanctuary came later. From the top of the ziggurat you can see what is left of the rich landscape of Sumer. Once fertile fields criss-crossed by canals, lined with palm groves, the territory of Uruk is now parched, wind-blown desert.[10]

Another candidate for the first full-fledged city, Eridu, lying about fifty miles southeast of Uruk, may have begun as a village as early as 5500 B.C. Eridu also featured a religious temple, this one dedicated to Enki, god of the primeval waters and of wisdom. It is possible that Eridu was an older site used mainly as a ceremonial center and that Uruk was the first actual urban center supporting a large population. Regardless of which settlement became a thriving city-state first, it is certain that the Sumerians believed that Eridu was the site of the original mound of creation, the primeval land thought to have risen from the sea at the beginning of time. They also held that Eridu was the home of the first king and the first civilized arts and crafts.

These and other prominent Sumerian cities—including Lagash, Ur, Larsa, and Nippur—engaged in commerce, trading foodstuffs, fabric and clothes, pottery, and other goods. Some of the trade routes extended northward into Akkad, in central Mesopotamia. In this more backward area, where people spoke a Semitic tongue rather than Sumerian, the cities were less prosperous and vied with one another for whatever bounty trickled in from the Sumerian heartland. Indeed, competition over trade routes and privileges are one reason that the cities of both Sumeria and Akkad periodically fought among themselves. Other major reasons included disputes over water rights and local territory. Typically, one city-state would amass considerable power and prestige and dominate most of the others for a generation or a century or so. Then the balance of power would shift and another city-state would rise to prominence.

KINGSHIP AND EMPIRE

Frequent threats to the integrity of the cities, as well as outright wars, must have contributed to the emergence of kings, strong figures charged with protecting their peoples.

As strong political-military rulers gained permanent control of the cities, it was perhaps inevitable that one of them, either from Sumer or Akkad, would try to conquer the entire region. Sargon of Akkad, who managed this feat and created the world's first known

Scholars think that this life-sized bronze head is a likeness of either Sargon of Akkad or his grandson, Naram-Sin.

from Kish, a city located a few miles east of Babylon on the northern bank of the Euphrates.

For Sargon, the road to empire began when the king of the Sumerian city of Uruk captured Kish. Apparently, Sargon and some followers managed to escape and soon afterward established the city of Akkad (or Agade), perhaps located about ten miles north of Babylon. Probably after rallying Akkadian forces from other cities, Sargon marched on Kish and dislodged the Sumerian intruder. Then, emboldened by his victory, Sargon headed southward and attacked and seized control of the Sumerian city-states one by one. His armies reached the Persian Gulf in the southeast and also moved northwestward into Syria; so for the first time in history, the lower and upper halves of Mesopotamia were united as one large political unit. This empire was successful for a while because Sargon and his immediate successors instituted policies that were "radically different than those of their predecessors," Saggs points out.

empire, was born about 2334 B.C. While he was a boy, an unknown number of Akkadian rulers managed to unite the central Mesopotamian city-states into a sort of national alliance of states (the structure of which remains uncertain). The adult Sargon became a royal official under one of these kings, who ruled

Unlike most earlier major rulers, Sargon was not content with mere [local kingship]. He wanted real rulership over the whole land. To this end, he [dismantled parts of] the walls of other cities to make future resistance ineffective; he installed citizens of his own capital, doubtless personal friends and perhaps kinsmen, as administrators in

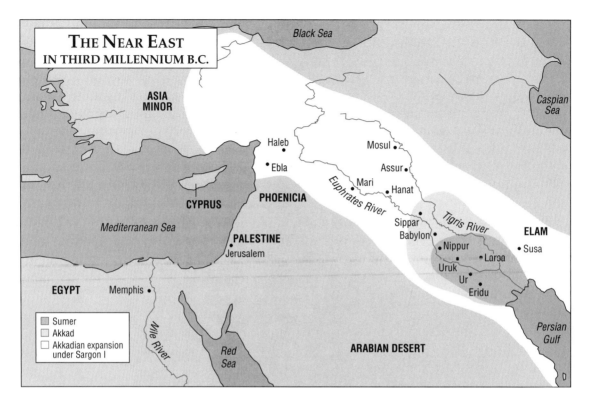

other city-states to preclude any independent policy; and he made seagoing vessels tie up at Agade, to gather control of all foreign trade into his own hands.[11]

THE EARLY MESOPOTAMIAN MILITARY

Sargon and his Akkadian heirs enforced these policies the same way imperialists have all through history—through military force. Ancient inscriptions suggest that they had at their disposal an army that numbered at least in the tens of thousands. And as Saggs says, they "were prepared to use overwhelming force, regardless of how many victims they killed, to deal with any city that stood in their way."[12] It appears

that Sargon's immediate successor, Rimush, was particularly ruthless. His inscriptions brag about killing tens of thousands of people and forcing thousands more into forced labor camps.

The specific military weapons and tactics employed by the armies of the Akkadian Sargonids and the other Mesopotamian strongmen who followed them had long been used on a small scale in Sumer and neighboring areas. The empire builders simply applied to them on a much larger scale.

Some idea of what a Sumerian battle formation was like during the era of Akkad's ascendancy is provided by a scene carved onto the famous stone Vulture Stele, which takes its name from its depiction of enemy dead being picked at by vultures. In the scene, the soldiers of the victorious army march over the bodies of their defeated enemies. Leading the triumphant troops is the king himself, who in another section of the stele rides in a battlewagon. These soldiers are of two types. Some are light infantrymen, who wear no armor and wield long spears and battle-axes. In contrast, the heavy infantrymen wear armor and helmets and stand in massed, closely packed ranks, each man holding up a large shield. The spears of the heavy infantrymen project through the spaces between the shields. Fighting in such a tight, specialized formation requires a lot of training, so it is likely that these men were part- or perhaps even full-time professional soldiers.

Such vehicles were solid-wheeled carts pulled by four donkeys or onagers (wild Asiatic asses); horses were not yet

This section of the Vulture Stele shows a group of infantrymen marching forward in tightly packed ranks, their spears projecting forward.

widely used in the Near East. The manner in which they were used on the battlefield is unclear. They were quite heavy and not very maneuverable, and donkeys and onagers are not fast runners; so the battle wagons were likely ineffective against masses of infantry. Perhaps, as scholar Stephen Bertman suggests, they might have been used occasionally "for a kamikaze-style attack on the enemy commander-in-chief."[13] For the most part,

though, they were probably used as "prestige" vehicles for chauffeuring the king and his officers to and from the battlefield.

More effective were the standard infantry weapons of the era. These included the heavy spear, used mainly for thrusting and stabbing rather than for throwing; the battle-ax, for slashing through helmets and skulls; and the dagger, used as a backup weapon. It appears that the bow and arrow was only rarely used at this time,

The well-preserved remains of the great Ziggurat of Nanna at Ur, in present-day Iraq. Nanna was a moon god widely worshiped in Mesopotamia.

partly because the bow did not yet have the power to shoot its missiles very far. Perhaps the most effective use of bows in the third millennium B.C. was during sieges when the defenders on city walls showered arrows down on attackers.

THE RISE AND FALL OF UR

Although the Akkadian Sargonids used these weapons and tactics extremely effectively, their empire was short-lived, especially in comparison with some of the empires that would later rise in the region of Mesopotamia. For reasons that are unclear, shortly after 2200 B.C. the Akkadian realm quickly fell apart. Perhaps its kings overextended themselves and tried to rule too many cities at once. Or maybe rebellions of their subject peoples took a deadly toll. Some evidence suggests that another factor consisted of repeated attacks by the Gutians, fierce tribesmen from the hills north of the Mesopotamian plains.

Whatever the reasons for Akkad's demise, in the century that followed political chaos was widespread. Among the competing, but not very organized, factions were the Gutians, Elamites (from the hill country directly north of the Persian Gulf), Amorites (from western Mesopotamia), and a few surviving Sumerian cites. Finally, in about 2112 B.C., Ur-Nammu, king of the Sumerian city of Ur, established a dynasty (family line of rulers) that amassed enough power to create a new empire, the second to rise in the region. Modern historians call it the Third Dynasty of Ur. It was somewhat smaller than the Sargonid realm, but its rulers brought renewed order and prosperity,

which had declined after the fall of Akkad.

Monumental architecture also prospered under the Ur dynasts. Ur-Nammu erected an enormous ziggurat that is still partially intact after the passage of more than four thousand years. "At its base," Samuel Kramer writes, "this gigantic structure of brickwork covers an area of 200 by 140 feet; its original three-terraced stages [levels] with their crowning shrine towered some 70 feet above the city."[14] Ur-Nammu also issued a law code, perhaps the first in history, before dying in battle against the Gutians.

Ur-Nammu's successors tried to enlarge the realm he had left them. But these remaining Ur dynasts—including Shulgi (who ascended the throne ca. 2094 B.C.), Amar-Sin (ca. 2046), Shu-Sin (ca. 2037), and Ibbi-Sin (ca. 2028)—had all they could do to manage the existing empire. They endured repeated assaults by Elamites from the east and Amorites from the west. Ur was eventually sacked by the Elamites (ca. 2004), marking the end of Sumerian power in Mesopotamia. The human slaughter in Ur (and perhaps in neighboring cities) was horrific, as revealed in a surviving text, *The Lamentation over the Destruction of Ur*:

> Dead men, not pottery, covered the approaches [to the city], the walls were gaping [i.e., filled with holes], the high gates, the roads were piled with dead. In the side streets, where feasting crowds would gather, scattered they [the bodies] lay. In all the streets and roadways bodies lay. In open fields that used to fill with dancers, they lay in heaps. The country's blood now filled its holes, like metal in a mold. Bodies dissolved—like fat left in the sun.[15]

THE INVENTION AND SPREAD OF WRITING

Though direct Sumerian political authority and administration was now a thing of the past, the influence of Sumerian culture was far from over. The social, political, religious, and artistic customs they had established became the model for later Mesopotamian cultures. Perhaps the most profound legacy the Sumerians left behind consisted of writing and literature. Sometime between 3300 and 3100 B.C., they had developed a complex writing system, an invention that had rapidly spread to other sections of the Near East and eventually beyond. The earliest technique used by scribes (an elite class of individuals trained to read and write) was simple but ingenious. First, they pressed pointed sticks into moist clay tablets. When the tablets dried and hardened, they became cumbersome but permanent records, the world's first versions of letters, account sheets, and books.

Eventually, this writing system featured mostly small wedge-shaped marks arranged in various combinations. Modern scholars came to call it "cuneiform" (after the Latin word *cuneus*, meaning "wedge shaped"). In all, Mesopotamian scribes used nearly six hundred separate cuneiform signs, which made writing and reading the language extremely difficult.

The vast majority of the thousands of cuneiform tablets discovered so far consist of dry administrative and financial records, including bills, accounts received, inventories, volumes of foodstuffs, and measures of land parcels.

Fortunately for later generations, however, some of Mesopotamia's cuneiform tablets have preserved actual literature, which is considerably varied in style. Among the surviving writings are myths about and hymns dedicated to the gods, tales of the adventures of human heroes, odes extolling the deeds and virtues of kings, lamentations for the fall of cities and rulers, poems that were sung at weddings and perhaps other important social gatherings, and proverbs and wise sayings.

THE ADVENTURES OF GILGAMESH

The most important examples of Sumerian literature were a group of myths about the creation and the exploits of some larger-than-life heroes, works that became the common heritage of all later Mesopotamian cultures. Among these heroes were Atrahasis and Gilgamesh. The more familiar of the two to Western readers is Atrahasis (also known as Utnapishtim), a wise and pious man who supposedly built a large ship, with which he and his family survived a great flood sent by the gods. Another Near Eastern people, the Hebrews, came to call him Noah (as did the Christians when they later adopted the Hebrew Old Testament).

By far the most influential of all the old Sumerian myths is the *Epic of Gilgamesh*. This hefty collection of early heroic tales and folklore was initially committed to writing by an unknown Mesopotamian scribe in about 2000 B.C. He wrote in the Akkadian language, but the content of the work, including the names of the characters and places, date from the era of Sumerian supremacy in the region. In fact, the title character may well have been a real Sumerian ruler of the dim past.

In Gilgamesh's timeless story, he starts out as the unpopular king of Uruk. Though a strong and valiant warrior, he is vain, insensitive, and sometimes brutal. Eventually, the city's elders appeal to the goddess Aruru, Uruk's patron deity, to find some way of humbling the king. She responds by creating a primitive man, Enkidu, who is just as strong and brave as Gilgamesh. At first, Enkidu lives with Gilgamesh in the latter's palace in the city, and the king's servants cut the wild man's hair and teach him manners. Enkidu soon becomes more civilized than Gilgamesh himself, partly because Aruru has given her creation a stronger sense of right and wrong than the king's. Gilgamesh and Enkidu eventually become inseparable friends. And under the influence of the former wild man, the king learns humility, sees the evil of his old ways, and becomes a model ruler.

Next, Gilgamesh and Enkidu have some heroic adventures in which they slay some dreadful monsters. But in time, they run afoul of the goddess Ishtar, who causes Enkidu to fall ill and die. Filled with grief, Gilgamesh contemplates the meaning of death and, hoping to save all future humans from that fate, decides to search for the secret of immortality. After a long and dangerous quest, however, he meets with failure. In the end, Gilgamesh learns the hard but valuable lesson that only the gods

FINDING GILGAMESH'S MISSING PIECES

English scholar and archaeologist George Smith produced the first English translation of the *Epic of Gilgamesh* in 1872. At the time, about fifteen of the work's thirty-five hundred lines were missing. A newspaper, the *Daily Telegraph*, financed an expedition to Iraq to find the missing lines, and fortunately, the team, led by Smith himself, accomplished this goal after only a few weeks of digging. Smith described the discovery in this excerpt from his 1875 book, *Assyrian Discoveries*:

"On the 14th of May . . . I sat down to examine the store of fragments of cuneiform inscriptions from the day's digging, taking out and brushing off the earth from the fragments to read their contents. On cleaning one of them I found to my surprise and gratification that it contained the greater portion of seventeen lines of inscription belonging to the first column of the Chaldean [Babylonian] account of the Deluge [great flood], and fitting into the only place where there was a serious blank in the story. When I had first published the account of this tablet I had conjectured that there were about fifteen lines wanting [lacking] in this part of the story, and now with this portion I was enabled to make it nearly complete."

Found in the palace of Sargon II, this statue shows the hero Gilgamesh holding a sword in one hand and a lion cub in the other.

are immortal; all human beings, no matter how powerful, good, or brave, must face death.

TRADITION AND CONTINUITY

Though in the tale the Sumerian character Gilgamesh could not break the chains of mortality, the story itself achieved a kind of *im*mortality by becoming Mesopotamia's national epic after the Sumerians were gone. In the same manner, Sumer's language and religion survived its decline. After 2000 B.C. the Sumerian language was no longer widely spoken. But it remained a sort of sacred and literary language used by priests and scholars (in the same way that Latin remained in use by churchmen and scholars after it ceased to be spoken). Meanwhile, later Mesopotamians adopted the Sumerian cuneiform writing system to their own languages.

These later peoples, including the Assyrians and Babylonians, also absorbed Sumerian religious ideas and gods. The

THE CREATION OF ENKIDU

In this excerpt from Stephanie Dalley's acclaimed recent translation of the Gilgamesh epic in *Myths from Mesopotamia,* the goddess Aruru creates Gilgamesh's nemesis, the wild man Enkidu.

"Aruru washed her hands, pinched off a piece of clay, and cast it out into open country. [From the clay] she created a primitive man, Enkidu the warrior. . . . His whole body was shaggy with hair. . . . His locks of hair grew luxuriant like grain. He knew neither people nor country; he was dressed as cattle are [i.e., without clothes]. With gazelles, he eats vegetation, with cattle, he quenches his thirst at the watering place. With wild beasts, he satisfies his need for water. A hunter . . . came face to face with him beside the watering place. He saw him on three successive days beside the watering place. The hunter looked at him, and was dumbstruck to see him. In perplexity, he went back to his house and was afraid, stayed mute, was silent."

leading Sumerian gods were An, ruler of the universe; Enlil, creator and ruler of Earth; Enki, god of the waters; and Enzu, Utu, and Inanna, deities of the moon, sun, and planet Venus, respectively. Later Mesopotamians borrowed these gods outright, sometimes changing their names. For example, the Babylonians identified their chief god, Marduk, with the Sumerian Enlil. Thus, when new Mesopotamian empires began to grow in what was once Sumer, little changed but the names of the kings and gods. For a long time to come, as in ages past, the overriding cultural concepts in the region would be tradition and continuity.

2 Rise of the Assyrians and Babylonians

Modern scholars assign the name Old Babylonian Period to the span of roughly four centuries (ca. 2000–1600 B.C.) that followed the collapse of the Third Dynasty of Ur. With the disappearance of central imperial control, the city-states of Mesopotamia became independent and disunited once again, and they frequently engaged in disputes and wars among themselves or with various peoples living in the highland regions surrounding the plains. From time to time, one of these states would suddenly burst from its home area, seize control of several of its neighbors, and enjoy a brief moment of expanded power and prestige. Then, beset by internal instability and external enemies, it would just as suddenly fall back to its former status.

Thus, the Old Babylonian Period was a time of intense rivalry and political opportunity in Mesopotamia. And as Gwendolyn Leick points out, in such an environment only the strongest and cleverest could enjoy survival and success:

> In the rapidly changing political climate, the most tenacious leaders also needed particular character traits in order to stay in the game. They had to be quick-witted, decisive, patient . . . charismatic . . . and ruthless. A tough

physique and a talent for military strategy also helped. Most important was an ability to communicate with all the different social groupings and find the right tone to address both pastoralist [rural] tribesmen and urban bureaucrats.[16]

The most successful of these opportunists and strongmen established new dynasties, in some cases planting the seeds for future empires. Most of these new dynasties were founded by Amorites, who spoke Akkadian; this is the main reason that the Sumerian language rapidly declined in this period. Amorites took over Ur, Larsa, Babylon, and other cities in southern and central Mesopotamia. Meanwhile, the Elamites (who spoke a tongue unrelated to any others in the Near East) continued to be a powerful presence in the southeast. And in northern Mesopotamia, on the upper reaches of the Tigris, other Amorite Akkadian speakers established a strong state centered in the city of Assur (or Ashur). Of the many city-states now competing in Mesopotamia, Assur and Babylon would prove to be the most successful; the Assyrians and Babylonians would be the major players in the region's affairs for more than a thousand years to come.

A New Dynasty at Assur

Of these two peoples, the Assyrians were first to assert themselves in a big way in the political rivalry of the early second millennium B.C. Before the Old Babylonian Period, Assur had been an obscure town that, along with many others, had been absorbed and ruled by the Sargonids and Ur dynasts. Dominated by these early imperialists, the local Assyrians dared not aspire to independence, much less imperial dreams of their own.

Yet when the Ur dynasts fell to the Elamites, Assur did become independent. And in time, one of the new political-military strongmen of the day saw the potential of creating a power base in the area. In 1813 B.C. Shamshi-Adad, apparently a military general of Amorite descent, overthrew the leaders of Assur and established a new dynasty there. Posterity would come to see it as the first important Assyrian family of rulers. Posterity has also been fortunate that in 1935 French excavators discovered some three hundred letters (written in cuneiform on stone tablets) constituting a lively correspondence between Shamshi-Adad and his sons. Thanks to these artifacts, more is known about these Assyrian monarchs than about most other national figures of the period.

One of Shamshi-Adad's letters tells how, when he first took power in Assur, he built an imposing temple to the old Sumerian god Enlil and invoked that deity's blessings. This wise move was part of a strategy used by almost all conquerors and monarchs in ancient times—claiming that one's ascension to the throne has been approved and blessed by divine authority. "Shamshi-Adad, king of the whole world, who built the temple of the god Assur," the letter begins,

> he whose name the gods Anum and Enlil uttered out of regard for [his]

The ruins of Assur, one of Assyria's capitals, are highly eroded from long exposure to the elements.

great deeds. . . . The temple of Enlil my lord, an awesome chapel, a mighty building, the seat of my lord Enlil, that stands securely built by the work of the builders, did I build in my city Assur. To the temple I gave a roof of cedar-logs. In the chambers I set up doors of cedar wood with inlays of silver and gold . . . and I sprinkled the foundation with cedar oil, oil of the best kind, honey and butter.[17]

SHAMSHI-ADAD'S CONQUESTS

Once he had consolidated his power base in Assur, Shamshi-Adad must have felt confident that he could create an empire like that of the legendary Sargonids. (By this time Sargon and his deeds had indeed faded into the realm of legend. It must be remembered that four centuries had elapsed from the fall of the Akkadian Empire to Shamshi-Adad's rise to power, a period nearly twice as long as the United States has existed as a nation.) The new Assyrian king's first foreign conquest was his seizure of the prosperous independent city-state of Mari, situated about 140 miles southwest of Assur. Shamshi-Adad placed his son Jamsah-Adad on Mari's throne. Then the father attacked and subdued the city-state of Ekallatum, on the Tigris south of Assur, and installed another son, Ishme-Dagan, as its ruler.

Next, Shamshi-Adad marched his forces toward the west and southeast. In the west he reached what is now Lebanon, on the Mediterranean coast. At the time and for many centuries afterward, Lebanon was

---

EARLY ASSYRIAN AGGRESSIONS

It appears that Shamshi-Adad and his sons almost constantly waged small-scale wars with their neighbors, always attempting to gain new territory. This is revealed by numerous excerpts from their letters, including these two examples (quoted in Jorgen Laessoe's *People of Ancient Assyria: Their Inscriptions and Correspondence*).

"Say to Jamsah-Adad: Thus says Shamshi-Adad your father. Having five days ago defeated the ruler of Qabra, now I have also defeated [the tribe] Ja'ilanum. I have also taken the town of Hibara. In this town I have made myself master of 300 of his [i.e., the ruler's] garrison troops and one of his sons. Rejoice!

Say to Jamsah-Adad: Thus says Ishme-Dagan, your brother. As soon as I had taken the towns of Tarram, Hatka, and Shunham, I turned against Hurara. This town I surrounded. I caused siege towers and battering-rams to be raised against it, and in the course of seven days I made myself master of it. Rejoice!"

---

the source of the high-quality cedar wood used for palaces and other large buildings in Assyria and Babylonia. The local rulers must not have had armies to compare with that of Shamshi-Adad, because they gave him tribute, gold and other valuable goods acknowledging their submission. Before returning to Assur, he put up a stele (stone marker) commemorating his expedition. The stele, which has survived, reads: "My great name and my memorial stele I set up in the country of Laban [Lebanon], on the shore of the Great Sea."[18]

Assyrian military expeditions in the southeast concentrated on conquering the state of Eshnunna, about 160 miles from Assur (and some forty miles north of present-day Baghdad). Eshnunna controlled the valley of the Diyala River, a major tributary of the Tigris. It was a strong independent state and evidently held its own against the invaders. Probably because so many of his troops were engaged in this operation, Shamshi-Adad did not attempt to attack another strong state lying southeast of Assur—Babylon; instead, he maintained a polite but cool and uneasy peace with its rulers.

THE ASCENDANCY OF HAMMURABI

These first, fairly small-scale Assyrian conquests came to a halt shortly after Shamshi-Adad died in 1781 B.C. His successor, his son Ishme-Dagan, likely thought that the nation would remain strong and that he would have no trouble continuing the military campaigns Shamshi-Adad had initiated. A letter to his brother Jamsah-Adad, who was still ruling Mari, reads in part:

I have ascended the throne of my father's house. This is why I have been extremely busy, and have not been able to send you news of my well-being. . . . You must not be anxious. Your throne is and will remain your throne. The gods Adad and Shamash I hold in my hand. The peoples from Elam and the man [i.e., the king] of Eshnunna I lead by the reins. . . . Let us swear a binding oath to each other . . . [and] maintain brotherly relationships with each other for all time.[19]

Not long after Jamsah-Adad received this letter, however, a series of unexpected events profoundly changed the face not only of Assyria but of all Mesopotamia. First, Jamsah-Adad was overthrown by a local Marian official named Zimrilim, and Mari regained its independence. Then, only a few years later, perhaps in 1759 B.C., Mari was almost completely destroyed by a Babylonian army. Soon afterward, the same army captured Assur and the other Assyrian cities.

The leader of these formidable forces was Hammurabi, the sixth king of an Amorite dynasty that had established itself in Babylon circa 1850 B.C. During the first several years of his reign, he had made alliances, or at least maintained good relations, with neighboring states, including Mari, Larsa, and Eshnunna. But in the late 1760s B.C., Hammurabi suddenly chose a path of war and conquest. "The new king of Babylon was not content merely to maintain an uneasy coexistence with his dangerous neighbors," says Samuel Kramer. "Driven by a desire to mold a deeply divided land into a unified state that . . . would

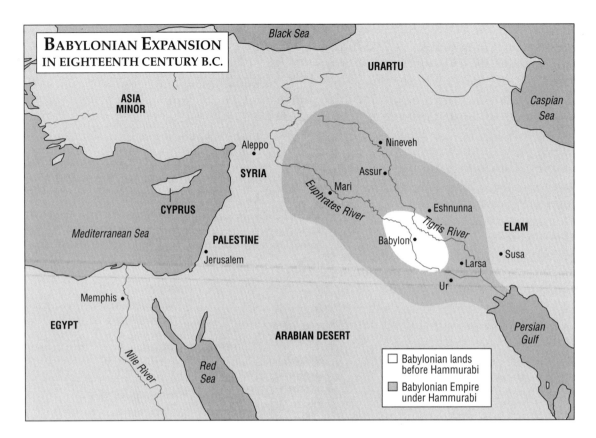

BABYLONIAN EXPANSION IN EIGHTEENTH CENTURY B.C.

Black Sea

URARTU

ASIA MINOR

Caspian Sea

Aleppo

Nineveh

SYRIA

Assur

Mari

Euphrates River

CYPRUS

Eshnunna

Tigris River

ELAM

Mediterranean Sea

PALESTINE

Babylon

Jerusalem

Susa

Larsa

Ur

Memphis

EGYPT

Persian Gulf

ARABIAN DESERT

Nile River

Red Sea

☐ Babylonian lands before Hammurabi

■ Babylonian Empire under Hammurabi

play a prominent role in the ancient world, Hammurabi proceeded to overwhelm and destroy his rivals one by one."[20]

First, Hammurabi captured Larsa, giving him control of most of southern Mesopotamia. Then he moved northwestward, took Eshnunna, and destroyed Mari. From there, he moved into the Assyrian heartland near the upper Tigris and overran Assur, Nineveh, and the other main Assyrian strongholds. Eventually, Hammurabi became the first ruler since Sargon of Akkad to achieve the glorious dream of a united Mesopotamia. The exact extent of this new Babylonian empire is somewhat unclear. Modern scholars believe that it stretched from the Persian Gulf in the southeast to the borders of

Syria and the Armenian foothills in the northwest.

"I Promoted the Welfare of the Land"

The inscriptions Hammurabi left behind boast of him as more than just a skilled military leader and conqueror. He seems to have been an able ruler and administrator who took an interest in a wide range of domestic, economic, and other affairs. Under his lead, for example, trade flourished throughout Mesopotamia, and as a result Babylon grew rich. He also maintained the old shrines and built new ones and ordered the construction of new irrigation channels. In the arts, he promoted traditional literature by having the old Sumerian creation myths recited at the New Year's festival of the Babylonian god Marduk. He also encouraged scholarly pursuits, including studies in mathematics.

In addition, seeing himself as an especially just ruler, Hammurabi issued a law code, which was based to some degree on earlier Sumerian and Akkadian models. Much of the slab of stone on which his scribes carved the code has survived. At the end of the list of laws, Hammurabi presented his rationale for compiling them: "Let a man who has been wronged and has a cause, go before my stele . . . and let him have my words inscribed on the monument read out."[21] It is revealing that the average person had to have a scribe "read out" the laws, which confirms other evidence suggesting that most people in the empire were illiterate.

However well meaning Hammurabi may have been in issuing his laws, they were not extensive or detailed enough to govern all aspects of society. Also, by modern standards, they were often quite harsh. "If a man committed robbery and was then caught," one reads, "he shall be put to death." Another says, "If a man has caused a slave . . . of the palace . . . to go out of the great gate [of the city], he shall be put to death."[22] Other offenses that invoked the death penalty included murder, falsely accusing someone of murder, engaging in sorcery, kidnapping, receiving stolen goods, breaking and entering a home, arson, and performing a government job poorly. For lesser offenses, the penalties were also extreme, ranging from breaking a limb or cutting off an ear or tongue to burning, near

drowning, whipping, confiscation of property, and exile.

It is unknown how effective these laws and penalties were in Mesopotamian society. More certain is that Hammurabi was a widely respected and feared ruler and that he fancied himself a great one. In one of his inscriptions, he bragged:

> I rooted out the enemy above and below; I made an end of war; I promoted the welfare of the land; I made the peoples rest in friendly habitations; I did not let anyone terrorize them. . . . I have governed them in peace; I have sheltered them in my strength.[23]

HITTITES, KASSITES, AND HURRIANS

The peace and shelter Hammurabi claimed to bestow on his subjects did not last long after he died in about 1750 B.C. Under the rule of his son, Samsu-iluna, many of the local peoples who had been brought into the Babylonian fold through conquest rebelled, and as had happened to the Mesopotamian empires of the past, this one rapidly began to crumble. One by one, the captured territories fell away and became independent once more, until Babylon was no more than a large but politically impotent city-state.

Meanwhile, events transpiring far to the north of Mesopotamia were about to affect that city-state in significant ways. Back in the 1700s B.C., during the glory days of Shamshi-Adad and Hammurabi, the people living in the central portion of Asia Minor had established a powerful military state. Known as Hatti, its capital was the city of Hattusas, near the Halys River. These Hittites, as they came to be called, began raiding southward and eventually set their sights on the riches of Syria. During the reign of the last ruler of Hammurabi's dynasty—Samsu-ditana—an ambitious Hittite king named Mursilis not only defeated Syria but also turned eastward and marched on Babylon, then the greatest metropolis in Mesopotamia. The city fell to Mursilis's forces about the year 1595 B.C. A surviving Hittite inscription of the period records, "He marched to Babylon and he destroyed Babylon . . . and brought back captives and possessions of Babylon to Hattusas."[24]

In retrospect, this military strike seems strange, particularly in light of what happened next. No sooner had the invaders triumphed than they suddenly withdrew and went back into Asia Minor, never to return, and the Kassites, crude and warlike highlanders from the Zagros Mountains of eastern Iran, swept onto the plain and occupied Babylon.

The journey from Hatti to Babylon was a long, expensive, and risky venture for an army of that era. Also, no matter how large his army, Mursilis certainly could not have hoped to occupy and maintain control over a territory that was both as vast as central Mesopotamia and so far away from his home base. Why, then, would he expend so much time and effort and then abruptly abandon his prize?

The answer may well lie with the threat posed by another powerful kingdom lying directly between Mesopotamia and Asia Minor. An ambitious and warlike people, the Hurrians, had recently established a large state, called Mitanni, centered on the upper reaches of the Tigris. Its capital, Washukanni, lay only about two hundred miles northwest of Assur. It appears that the Hurrians wanted to build an empire of their own at the expense of their Mesopotamian, Syrian, and Hittite neighbors. Thus, as Australian scholar Trevor Bryce suggests, Mursilis's expedition to Babylon

arose from an alliance between the Hittites and the Kassites, the incentive for the Hittites being the rich spoils of Babylon, and for the Kassites the prospect of creating a new ruling dynasty in the city. A Hittite-Kassite alliance might also have helped offset the ever-present threat of Hurrian political and military expansion. . . . The Babylonian expedition may have been undertaken by Mursili not only for booty, but also to gain future Kassite support . . . against the Hurrian menace in the region.[25]

As it turned out, the Hurrians did prove a threat, but not to Hatti. In the 1400s B.C., Mitanni conquered the Assyrian cities of northern Mesopotamia, which were forced to give their allegiance to the warlords of Washukanni. In the meantime, the Kassite nobles who had taken control of Babylon were mightily impressed by refined Babylonian culture. And within only two or three generations, they were thoroughly absorbed and "Babylonianized"; they even gave up their native language in favor of the Akkadian dialect spoken in Babylon.

A STRICT NEW LAW CODE

The law code of Hammurabi, which was based in part on earlier Sumerian and Akkadian versions, influenced the justice systems of many later Mesopotamian peoples. These excerpts (from Robert F. Harper's translation of the code) are from the section dealing with personal injury and manslaughter.

195. If a son strikes his father, they shall cut off his hand.

196. If a man destroys the eye of another man, they shall destroy his eye.

197. If he break another man's bone, they shall break his bone.

198. If he destroy the eye of a client or break the bone of a client, he shall pay one mina of silver.

199. If he destroy the eye of a man's slave or break the bone of a man's slave, he shall pay one-half his price [i.e., one-half the amount the owner paid for the slave].

200. If a man knock out a tooth of a man of his own rank, they shall knock out his tooth. . . .

206. If a man strike another man in a quarrel and wound him, he shall swear, 'I struck him without intent,' and he shall pay for the physician.

207. If he die as a result of the blow, he shall swear (as above), and if the man was a free man, he shall pay one-half mina of silver.

Large portions of Hammurabi's law code are carved onto this stele.

The ruins of the colossal Lion's Gate, one of five main gates that led into the Hittite capital of Hattusas (near modern Boghazkoy, Turkey).

NEW MILITARY INNOVATIONS

Lasting more than four centuries, the dynasty of the Kassite rulers turned out to be the longest and most stable that Babylon had ever experienced. Efficient and persuasive, they managed to bring most of the city-states of southern and central Mesopotamia under Babylonian control or influence. Now the dominant political entity in Mesopotamia, Babylonia became less of a group of cities bound together in an empire and more of a country made up of many cities.

Part of the reason for this stability was that Babylon's rulers did not waste their resources trying to create a huge empire beyond Mesopotamia's borders. In fact, the new international situation they faced made such a course very daunting, expensive, and risky. The powerful states of Mitanni and Hatti controlled Assyria and the lands north and west, and in the southwest, the

Egyptians had recently burst out of their own homeland and taken control of Palestine. All of these foreign powers posed a serious potential threat to Babylonian territory and interests; moreover, each had developed the capability of moving armies quickly over long distances. As Leick puts it, "A new era was beginning which drew the world of the whole ancient Near East closer together. This was not least due to technological changes in warfare."[26]

Indeed, during the last years of the Old Babylonian Period, three major military innovations had developed in the Near East. (Or they had filtered in from western Asia; the origin of these new ideas is still disputed.) First came the widespread domestication of the horse, which was more often harnessed to chariots than ridden. Second was the perfection of woodworking techniques that allowed the construction of wheels with spokes and the manufacture of lightweight chariot bodies. The combination of faster draft animals and lighter vehicles made it possible to launch attacks by massed chariots on the battlefield. Thus, Babylonia, Mitanni, Hatti, and Egypt all developed chariot corps capable of charging and breaking up infantry formations.

The third military innovation was a deadlier version of the simple bow. Called the composite bow, it was made by combining various separate materials to create a bow of greater elasticity and power. The four main materials in the new bow were wood, animal horn, animal tendons (sinew),

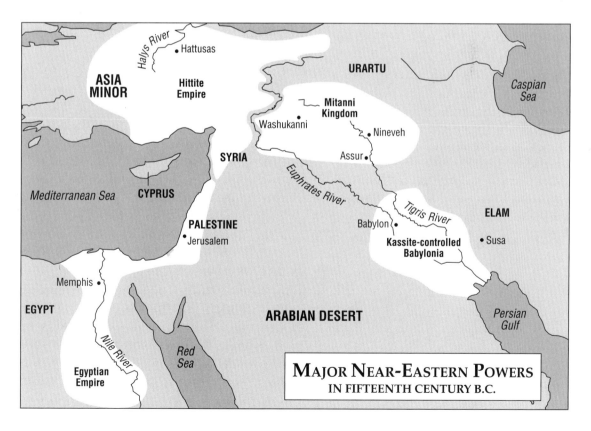

MAJOR NEAR-EASTERN POWERS
IN FIFTEENTH CENTURY B.C.

and glue. Even the wooden portions might be composed of two, three, or four varieties of wood, each having a certain desired pliability and combined in a carefully planned fashion. The harder animal horn was used in spots that needed more rigidity, and the sinews were applied to the back of the bow to increase its propulsive (springing) power. The result was a bow that could fire an arrow up to six hundred yards, though any sort of accuracy could be maintained only up to two hundred yards at most. Still, this was far superior to the performance of an ordinary bow. "The effective development of the practical composite bow," historian Trevor Watkins writes, "introduced a rapid fire missile delivery system necessary for mounting on the fast new chariots."[27]

ASSYRIA'S REBIRTH

The adoption and widespread proliferation of these effective new weapons systems made it almost inevitable that they would be used. Circa 1482 B.C., for instance, the Egyptian pharaoh Thutmose III employed his chariot corps in a decisive defeat of the Mitannians at Megiddo, in Palestine. Eventually, such large-scale military battles and campaigns brought about a major realignment of the power structure of the Near East, including Mesopotamia. About 1380 B.C., an ambitious Hittite king, Suppiluliumas I, moved southward and attacked Mitanni, which had lately grown weak and vulnerable thanks to civil unrest within its own borders. The Hittites drove into Mitanni's heartland, sacked Washukanni, and virtually erased this once-powerful kingdom from the historical map. That left Assyria, which in recent centuries had lapsed into obscurity under Mitannian occupation, once more independent and a potential rival to Kassite-ruled Babylonia.

Assyria quickly realized that potential as it now began its first great period of expansion and empire (in what modern scholars call the Middle Assyrian Period). In about 1365 B.C., an aggressive Assyrian king named Assuruballit I seized large sections of former Mitannian territory. Thereafter, his nation's foreign and military policy operated on three major fronts. The first consisted of the broad arc of foothills, ranging from the border of Hatti in the northwest, eastward through Armenia to the Zagros Mountains. The Assyrians conducted frequent small-scale raids into these northern hills, taking human captives, horses, and other booty.

Assyria's second major front was the ever-changing border with Babylonia in the southeast. Numerous confrontations between the two powers culminated in the capture of Babylon by the vigorous Assyrian monarch Tukulti-Ninurta I (ruled ca. 1244–1208 B.C.) some time early in his reign. "I forced Kashtilash, king of Babylonia, to give battle," he boasted in a surviving inscription.

> I brought about the defeat of his armies . . . and captured Kashtilash, the Kassite king. His royal neck I trod on with my feet, like a footstool. Stripped and bound, before Assur my lord, I brought him. Sumer and Akkad to its farthest border, I brought under my sway.[28]

Victory over their longtime rival naturally filled the Assyrians with pride and

CONQUEST BY DIVINE RIGHT

Tiglathpileser I extended Assyria's borders farther than any other ruler of his era, fulfilling what he believed was his duty to the gods—to conquer and expand in their name. This sense of divine purpose is clear in this surviving text from his reign (quoted in volume 1 of Daniel D. Luckenbill's *Ancient Records of Assyria and Babylonia*).

"Assur and the great gods, who have made my kingdom great, and who have bestowed might and power as a gift, commanded that I should extend the boundary of their land, and they entrusted to my hand their mighty weapons, the storm of battle. Lands, mountains, cities, and princes, the enemies of Assur, I have brought under my sway, and have subdued their territories. . . . Unto Assyria I added land, unto her peoples, peoples. I enlarged the frontier of my land, and all their lands I brought under my sway."

satisfaction, but they were not able to maintain control of Babylonia for very long. First, the Babylonian nobles rebelled and regained control of their territory. Then, in about 1165 B.C., a strong Elamite king, Kutir-Nakkhunte, took Babylon, eradicating the Kassite line of rulers for good and carrying the most sacred statue of the god Marduk back to the Elamite capital of Susa.

On its third major military front, the western corridor to Syria and the Mediterranean Sea, Assyria launched relentless offensives. A military expedition led by the Assyrian king Adad-nirari I (ca. 1305–1274 B.C.) reached Carchemish, in northern Syria, less than ninety miles from the sea. And Adad-nirari's immediate successor, Shalmaneser I, accomplished the same feat. The most outstanding gains in Assyria's first period of empire building were those of Tiglathpileser I (ca. 1115–ca. 1077 B.C.), who expanded

the realm on all three of its major fronts. He fulfilled the long-held Assyrian dream of reaching the Mediterranean coast (accomplished briefly by Shamshi-Adad seven centuries before) and he gained tremendous prestige by capturing Babylon.

Yet these gains proved only temporary. Tiglathpileser was assassinated in about 1077 B.C., and his successors were unable to maintain the cohesion of so large a realm inhabited by so many diverse peoples. In a little more than a century, the empire shrank until all that remained was its core—the traditional Assyrian heartland centered around Assur and Nineveh. As posterity has shown, however, Assyria was not dead; it had only slipped into a sort of hibernation. In time it would reawaken and in a mighty burst of zeal create a Mesopotamian empire that would be feared far and wide.

Chapter

3 The Assyrian Empire Reaches Its Zenith

In the years following the death of the Assyrian monarch Tiglathpileser I, Assyrian power and territory shrank. Mesopotamia as a whole also entered a period of decline, becoming a sort of disjoined power vacuum in which small, weak states struggled for survival and accomplished little. The Babylonians were back in control of their great city, having recently managed to eject the Elamites. But the next few Babylonian royal dynasties featured unremarkable rulers who did no more than maintain the status quo in the region.

Meanwhile, new peoples were entering the Mesopotamian melting pot. The most prominent, the Aramaeans, originally tribal peoples of the Syrian deserts, set up some small kingdoms in Syria and along the Mediterranean coast. Some Aramaeans also migrated in large bands into northern and western Mesopotamia and settled wherever they could. Their language, Aramaic, was a Semitic tongue that used a simple alphabet rather than the complex and difficult cuneiform system. So it is not surprising that Aramaic spread rapidly and soon replaced Akkadian as Mesopotamia's lingua franca, or universal language.

The spread of the Aramaeans added to the political fragmentation of Mesopotamia.

But this uncertain and sometimes unstable situation was not destined to last long. There had always been a tendency toward centralized rule in the region, and it was only a matter of time before one local group chose the familiar path of empire.

At the time it seemed unlikely that the Assyrians would be the ones to take that fateful path. After all, by the end of the tenth century B.C., their nation had reached its lowest ebb of power and prestige since it had first become independent over a thousand years before. Its territory had also declined. Assyria now consisted of a small slab of land, measuring barely one hundred miles long and fifty miles wide, centered near the junction of the Tigris and Upper Zab Rivers.

Yet even in these lean years, Assyrian rulers remained stubborn diehards who refused to give up the dream of reviving their ancestors' glories. Beginning with Adad-nirari II, who reached the throne circa 911 B.C., a series of strong kings slowly but steadily transformed their tiny, bedraggled nation into the largest, most feared empire the world had yet seen. Their military campaigns often took the form of religious crusades undertaken in the name of the gods. And this became a justification for employing any means, no matter how harsh or brutal, to achieve success. Indeed, the Assyrians became infamous for their systematic cruelty. Nahum, a Hebrew prophet, later recalled with a shudder:

> The crack of the whip, and the rumble of the wheel, galloping horse and bounding chariot! Horsemen charging, flashing sword and glittering spear, hosts of the slain, heaps of corpses, dead bodies without end—they stumble over the bodies![29]

ARMED MIGHT AND TERROR TACTICS

This new national policy of aggression and brutal strong-arm methods is clearly reflected in the inscriptions of the man who revived Assyria's imperial dreams—Adad-nirari II. One reads: "Powerful in battle, who overthrows cities, who burns the mountains of the lands, am I. Strong hero, who consumes his enemies, who burns up the wicked and the evil, am I." Using a combination of armed might and terror tactics, the king drove the Aramaeans out of the Tigris valley and recaptured some of Assyria's lost cities in the plains west of the Tigris. "The defeat of the desert folk, the Aramaeans, was accomplished," he declared.

> The old city of Apku, which the kings who went before me had built, had fallen [in]to decay and was turned to a mound of ruins. That city I rebuilt. . . . I made it beautiful, I made it splendid, I made it greater than it had been before.[30]

The Assyrian kings who followed Adad-nirari consistently adopted this theme of "greater than before." Each made an effort to glorify himself and the god Assur through military deeds and large-scale building programs. And as each new king launched his nearly

---

A KING BRAGS OF HIS ATROCITIES

The systematic use of cruelty, terror, and atrocities by Assyrian kings is documented by their own annals. This excerpt from an inscription of King Assurnasirpal (quoted in volume 1 of Daniel Luckenbill's *Ancient Records of Assyria and Babylonia*) is a typical example.

"I captured the city; 600 of their warriors I put to the sword; 3,000 captives I burned with fire; I did not leave a single one among them alive to serve as a hostage. Hulai, their governor, I captured alive. Their corpses I formed into pillars [piles]; their young men and maidens I burned in the fire. Hulai . . . I flayed [skinned], his skin I spread upon the wall of the city . . . [and] the city I destroyed."

yearly military campaigns, he added a little more territory and a few new towns to the growing Assyrian realm. Many of these captured territories became official provinces, each ruled by an Assyrian governor appointed by the king. In this way, an empire with complex administrative machinery gradually emerged.

This empire had many strong and effective rulers. Though Adad-nirari achieved considerable success, his deeds paled in comparison to those of several of his successors. The first really great monarch of the new Assyria was Assurnasirpal II, who acquired the throne circa 883 B.C. About six years later, he marched his forces westward, hoping to do what no other Assyrian monarch had done since Tiglathpileser I more than two centuries before—reach the shores of the Mediterranean Sea. Assurnasirpal first fought his way through Aramaean-held territory until he reached Carchemish, on the west bank of the upper Euphrates. His detailed annals, many of which have survived, list battles, sieges, and many atrocities inflicted on enemies. These atrocities included cutting off noses, ears, fingers, and other mutilations, impaling some victims on sharp stakes, and entombing others inside palace walls.

THE EFFICIENT ASSYRIAN MILITARY

The conquests of Assurnasirpal and his successors would not have been possible without a well-organized and efficient army. Indeed, a strong army became the primary instrument of Assyrian power.

At first, its ranks were filled mostly by a levy (draft) of native Assyrians, who served on a campaign and then returned to their farming or other jobs. In time, as more foreign peoples came under the king's control, vassal rulers were obliged to supply men for the army's auxiliary units; some mercenaries (hired foreign troops) were also used.

The king was the army's commander in chief. An assistant, the *tartanu*, or "field marshal," oversaw the nitty-gritty of military organization and field operations. Under the *tartanu* were commanders of units of 1,000, 200, 100, 50, and 10 men each. And chariots were grouped into squadrons of 50, each with its own commander.

Many of the weapons and tactics of the new Assyrian army were similar to those used in the late second millennium B.C. The main offensive weapon remained the composite bow, which was usually employed in a tactical field unit known as the archer-pair. As the name suggests, it consisted of two men. The first man bore a large shield to protect against incoming arrows and other missiles; the second was the bowman, who huddled with his companion behind the shield and fired off volleys of arrows. Rows of hundreds or thousands of these pairs, who moved forward in unison during a battle, made up the mainstay of the Assyrian infantry. Chariots featured a similar arrangement— a driver and archer standing behind a protective screen mounted on the vehicle's front.

Assurnasirpal's successors used this well-oiled military machine almost relentlessly, either to conquer new lands

A section of a stone relief shows an archer-pair in action. Dating from the ninth century B.C., the relief was found in Assurnasirpal II's palace at Nimrud.

or to put down rebellions by peoples already subject to the empire. His son, Shalmaneser III (ca. 858–824 B.C.), for example, campaigned on all three of the nation's traditional fronts. He led Assyrian forces to the Persian Gulf in the south, the Zagros range in the east, and Palestine in the west. Following Shalmaneser on the throne was his son,

Shamshi-Adad V. He and the next few Assyrian kings spent most of their reigns quelling rebellions by the realm's subject peoples.

Then came Tiglathpileser III (ruled ca. 744–727 B.C.), one of Assyria's greatest monarchs and imperialists. He instituted a series of major administrative and military reforms, including replacing the system of

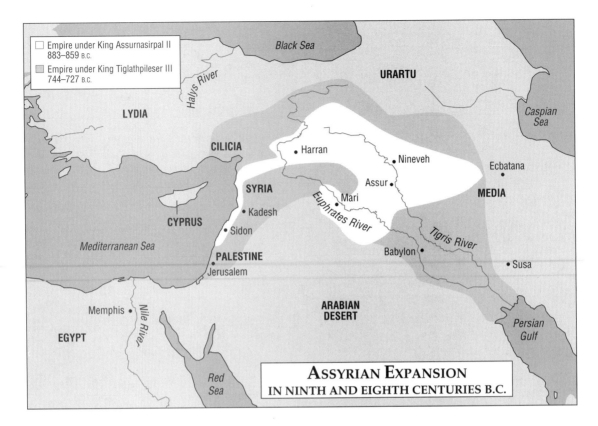

Black Sea

URARTU

Halys River

LYDIA

Caspian Sea

CILICIA

• Harran

↗ Nineveh

Ecbatana
•

SYRIA

Assur •

MEDIA

• Mari

Euphrates River

• Kadesh

CYPRUS

• Sidon

Tigris River

Mediterranean Sea

Babylon •

PALESTINE

• Susa

Jerusalem

Memphis •

Nile River

ARABIAN
DESERT

Persian
Gulf

EGYPT

Red
Sea

ASSYRIAN EXPANSION
IN NINTH AND EIGHTH CENTURIES B.C.

part-time soldiers with a permanent, full-time professional army. With this new army, Tiglathpileser assaulted and annexed most of Syria, fought the Medes and other hill peoples in the Zagros Mountains, and seized half of Israel.

ASCENDANCY OF SARGON II

Though impressive in their own time, Tiglathpileser's reforms and conquests only foreshadowed what soon became Assyria's greatest imperial age. The royal architects of that age were Sargon II, who reigned from about 722 to 705 B.C., and his three immediate successors—Sennacherib, Esarhaddon, and Assurbanipal. Collectively referred to by modern

historians as the Sargonids (not to be confused with the Akkadian Sargonids of a previous era), they are the best documented of any Mesopotamian rulers. The realm they carved out encompassed the entire courses of the Tigris and Euphrates Rivers, as well as parts of the Zagros range in the east, Armenia (then called Urartu) in the north, Asia Minor in the northwest, and Palestine in the west.

The manner in which this expansion was accomplished can be seen in the example of Sargon's conquest of Urartu (part of which had rebelled against Assyrian rule), beginning in 714 B.C. His annals vividly capture the rugged, dangerous trek of his army as it marched northward toward enemy territory:

I directed the line of march into the mountains. They were high mountains covered with all kinds of trees, whose surface was a jungle, whose passes were frightful, over whose area shadows stretch as in a cedar forest, the traveler of whose paths never sees the light of the sun . . . on whose sides gorges and precipices yawn, to look at which with the eyes, inspires fear; its road was too rough for chariots to mount, bad for horses, and too steep to march foot soldiers over. With [a] quick and keen understanding . . . I had my men carry mighty pickaxes . . . and they shattered the side of the high mountain . . . making a good road.[31]

Eventually, the Assyrians approached the valley in which Urartu's king, Ursa, was waiting with his own army. The only way to enter the valley was to climb an ice-covered mountain ridge, and Sargon himself led the way, scaling the cliffs

SKILL IN SIEGE TACTICS

Because they attacked and captured so many cities over the centuries, the Assyrians became very adept at siege tactics. In this excerpt from an article in John Hackett's *Warfare in the Ancient World*, noted historian D.J. Wiseman describes some of these tactics.

"A ramp or causeway of piled up earth, rubble or wood enabled the attacker to gain closer access to the upper, more penetrable and fragile walls. A battering ram was brought up by animal traction and then manhandled into position. This formidable weapon was a ram of metal-tipped wood housed in a wooden framework shielded by a covering. It was propelled on wheels or foot to dislodge the upper brickwork [of the walls] or smash down gateways or weak places. Attempts by defenders to set fire to these machines and the ramp by pouring burning oil or torches down on them usually failed, for the Assyrians devised contraptions to dowse the canopy with water. . . . Where the objective lay by a river, the Assyrians used a siege tower. Constructed upstream and floated into position, this gave a field of fire down onto the defenders within the walls. . . . Meanwhile sappers [miners], covered by bowmen and shields, attempted to tunnel and undermine the walls. . . . While a siege was in progress, the Assyrians devastated the surrounding countryside to cut off [the defenders'] forays for food."

while his attendants lugged his chariot and weapons. Descending into the valley, the Assyrians assembled and attacked, sending Ursa and his troops into panicked flight. Sargon's forces then gave chase and slaughtered many stragglers, after which the Assyrians terrorized Urartu by burning many towns, crops, and forests.

Sargon also fought on Assyria's southern front. Aided by the Elamites, Merodach-baladan, leader of the Chaldeans (Aramaeans living in what was once Sumer, near the Persian Gulf), had suddenly seized Babylon's throne. Sargon struggled against the Babylonians and Elamites for eleven years. And finally, in about 710 B.C., he was successful. Merodach-baladan fled to Elam, and Sargon entered Babylon in triumph.

In the short periods between his military campaigns, Sargon concentrated on large-scale building projects. At first he held court at Nimrud (north of Assur), but eventually he decided to create a new palace in a completely new city. In about 717 B.C. he laid the first foundations at Dur-Sharrukin (meaning "Sargon's fortress"), then a virgin site about fifteen miles northeast of Nineveh. His inauguration inscription reads: "For me, Sargon, who dwells in this palace, may he [the god Assur] decree as my destiny, eternal life."[32]

SENNACHERIB ATTACKS BABYLON

It turned out that eternal life was not in the cards for Sargon, who died about a year or two after inaugurating his new city and palace. Succeeding him was his son, Sennacherib (ruled ca. 704–681 B.C.), who wanted to make the already large realm even larger. First, however, he had

A stone relief shows an Assyrian army laying siege to the fortified Hebrew town of Lachish.

The Assyrian king Sennacherib holds audience in his encampment during the siege of Lachish. The city's leaders eventually paid Sennacherib to leave.

to devote his attention to several rebellions, which frequently plagued the powerful but widely unpopular Assyrian monarchs. First, the Chaldean usurper Merodach-baladan seized Babylon a second time. Then he convinced the rulers of Judah, Sidon, Ekron, and several other Palestinian states to rebel against Assyria.

Sennacherib dealt with the Babylonian problem first. He drove Merodach-baladan away and eventually sacked the city. "The city and its houses . . . I destroyed, I devastated, I burned with fire," Sennacherib boasted in an inscription. "Through the midst of that city I dug canals, I flooded its site with water."[33] The Assyrian king then turned his wrath on rebellious Palestine. Many people today are familiar with this campaign because parts of it are described in some detail in the Bible. The second book of Chronicles, for example, states:

Sennacherib, king of Assyria, who was besieging Lachish [south of Jerusalem] with all his forces, sent his servants to Jerusalem to Hezekiah, king of Judah, and to all the people of Judah . . . [saying] "On what are you relying, that you stand siege in Jerusalem. . . . Do you not know what I and my fathers have done to all the peoples of other lands?"[34]

Yet somehow the Hebrews in Jerusalem managed to outlast the Assyrian besiegers. Sennacherib finally agreed to withdraw in return for Hezekiah's pledge to pay heavy tribute (including his precious harem of wives).

Although such warfare occupied much of Sennacherib's time, he also expended considerable resources in enlarging and beautifying his capital city, Nineveh. His so-called Palace Without Rival, erected in the northern part of the town, was particularly noteworthy. According to his annals: "The former palace I greatly enlarged. I finished it and splendidly adorned it; to the amazement of all peoples I filled it with costly equipment."[35]

ASSYRIA'S GOLDEN AGE OF ART

Among the splendid trappings Sennacherib and many other Assyrian kings installed in their palaces were magnificent carved stone bas-reliefs that decorated the walls. These sculptures represent Assyria's chief artistic contribution to Mesopotamian culture. Especially numerous and striking were the ones carved during the era of the Sargonids,

making the seventh century B.C. a golden age of wall sculpture. In room after room, corridor after corridor of each palace, many thousands of feet of reliefs bore detailed scenes of the lives and exploits of the reigning monarchs. In some of the surviving panels, they can be seen dining in picturesque gardens laden with fruit trees; in others, they hunt lions or receive tribute from vassals; and in still others, they lead their armies in battle. "Sieges and battles" in these sculptures, "at times had almost a sense of space," Chester Starr observes,

and in the scenes of hunting, animals were shown with more realism than had ever before been achieved. Here the artists gave a vivid sense of motion, even at times of pity for the dying lions or wild asses; in other scenes the king, with fringed robe, long curled beard, and heavy shoulders and legs, was a static but powerful figure. Not until we come to Roman imperial art shall we find again artists who concentrated upon seizing the specific quality of individual historical events.[36]

This artistic depiction of historical events was most vivid in Sennacherib's palace at Nineveh. Here, modern excavators unearthed hundreds of feet of exquisite reliefs showing that king fighting his enemies, marching in a victory parade, feasting in the palace, and so forth. The various events and scenes are depicted in a formal, sometimes exaggerated manner, as one would expect from works meant to be a combination of art and propaganda. Yet the artists went to great pains to capture the court customs, costumes, architecture, social rankings, weapons, military tactics, religious rituals, musical instruments, and other aspects of real life in meticulous detail.

Assyrian artists also created many stunning painted scenes. Some adorned the brightly colored glazed bricks used to decorate the temples and palaces, while others were done on plaster, becoming attractive wall murals in both public buildings and private residences. In addition, Assyrian artisans turned out beautiful metal artifacts, including bronze, silver, and gold plates, drinking vessels, and ornaments. And their work in sculpted ivory was equally fine.

ESARHADDON'S EXPLOITS

Sennacherib's new palace at Nineveh was full of fine artistic creations. But like his father, he did not live long enough to really enjoy his proud new residence. Sennacherib was assassinated by his own sons in 681 B.C., and the youngest of the brood, Esarhaddon, took the throne after a brief power struggle with his equally ambitious brothers.

Esarhaddon's eleven-year reign was one of the most unusual of all the Assyrian kings. This was partly because he shrewdly used diplomacy to maintain a state of relative peace throughout most of his vast empire. That left him more time to get involved in constructive enterprises rather than in the almost constant warfare that had preoccupied his predecessors. For example, his first major act was to rebuild Babylon, which his father had so badly damaged. This enormous project continued throughout his reign, and the results were a larger, more splendid city and a new spirit of reconciliation between Babylonians and Assyrians. "I summoned all of my artisans and the people of Babylonia in their totality," one of his inscriptions reads.

CURSED BY THE GODS

Assyrian kings often left behind curses to discourage would-be defacers of their monuments. This one (quoted from volume 1 of Daniel Luckenbill's *Ancient Records of Assyria and Babylonia*) is by Adad-nirari I (reigned ca. 1300 B.C.).

"Whoever blots outs my name and writes his own name in its place, or breaks my memorial stele, or consigns it to destruction, or throws it into the river, or covers it with earth, or burns it in the fire . . . or if anyone because of these curses sends a hostile foe or an evil enemy . . . and has him seize it . . . may Assur, the mighty god . . . look upon him in great anger, and curse him with an evil curse. His name, his seed, his kith and kin, may they [the gods] destroy from the land."

In choice oil, honey, butter, wine . . . I laid its [the city's] foundation walls. I raised the headpad to my own head and carried it [i.e., as a symbolic gesture he carried the first load of stone himself]. . . . I built [Babylon] anew, I enlarged [it], I raised [it] aloft, I made [it] magnificent. The images of the great gods I restored and had them replaced in their shrines to adorn them forever. . . . The sons of Babylon . . . their clientship I established anew.[37]

This immense gesture of goodwill by Esarhaddon won him the lasting friendship of most Babylonians, an unprecedented turn of events in the long history of animosity between the two peoples.

However, Esarhaddon's goodwill toward Babylonia was by no means an indication that he was a soft-hearted ruler who had abandoned the harsh methods of his ancestors. When provoked, he could be both tough and brutal, as demonstrated by his treatment of the Palestinian city of Sidon, which rebelled against him. Quickly crushing the insurrection, Esarhaddon executed Sidon's king, demolished the city, and deported all of its surviving inhabitants to Assyria. These ruthless acts set the desired example, and for several years to come the small states along the Mediterranean coast remained quiet and obedient.

The entire Assyrian Empire became relatively quiet, in fact. This rare interlude seemed to Esarhaddon to be an opportune time to realize a goal that many Assyrian

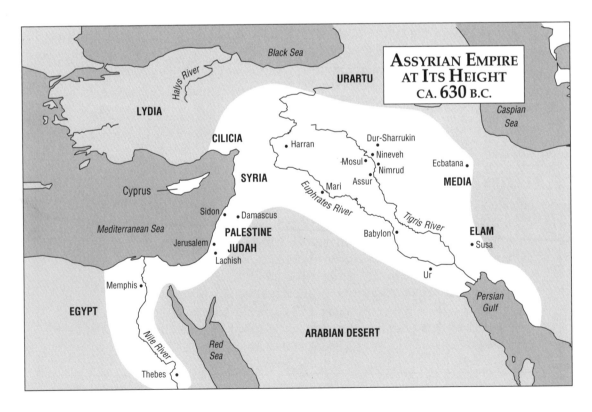

ASSYRIAN EMPIRE AT ITS HEIGHT CA. 630 B.C.

kings had only dreamed of—the conquest of Egypt. Almost as old as Mesopotamia, Egypt had once been a strong nation and empire. In recent centuries, however, it had grown weak and vulnerable. So Esarhaddon invaded Egypt in 671 B.C. and in less than a month captured its capital, Memphis, and most of the countryside surrounding it. About the Egyptian king, Taharqa, Esarhaddon recorded:

> Without cessation I slew multitudes of his men, and him I smote five times with the point of my javelin. . . . Memphis, his royal city, in half a day, with mines, tunnels, assaults, I besieged, I captured . . . I burned with fire. His queen, his harem, his . . . sons and daughters, his property and his goods, his horses, his cattle, his sheep, in countless numbers, I carried off to Assyria.[38]

Though his Egyptian expedition had been a success, Esarhaddon's governors had trouble maintaining order and control in the conquered country. Two years after the bulk of the Assyrian army had departed from Egypt, Taharqa returned with many followers, recaptured Memphis, and organized a large-scale rebellion. Esarhaddon hurriedly mounted an expedition to put down this revolt. But on his way to Egypt, he died unexpectedly, and his son, the crown prince Assurbanipal, succeeded him.

THE WRATH OF ASSURBANIPAL

When he ascended the throne in about 668 B.C., Assurbanipal inherited from his father the Assyrian Empire at its largest territorial extent. The immense realm stretched from the Nile valley in the southwest to central Armenia in the north, a distance of more than a thousand miles, and from the Mediterranean coast in the west to the shores of the Persian Gulf in the east, a distance of some seven hundred miles.

Yet, though huge, the empire was potentially unstable. At the moment, Egypt was in open rebellion, and Assurbanipal realized that other subject peoples might follow the Egyptians' lead at any moment. The best course seemed to be to crush the rebels as quickly as possible to set an example. So the king marched his army to Egypt, where, according to his annals, Taharqa and his own troops met the Assyrian host in open battle:

> With the help of Assur . . . [and] the great gods . . . who advance at my side, I defeated his army in a battle on the open plain. . . . The terrible splendor of [the gods] Assur and Ishtar overcame him and he went mad. . . . He forsook Memphis and fled to Thebes [a city far to the south].[39]

For the next several years, the defeated Egyptians continued to give Assurbanipal trouble as they continued launching rebellions. One rebel leader, Psamtik, even managed to drive the Assyrian occupation forces out of the country and well into Palestine. It is almost certain that Assurbanipal planned to punish this affront to him and his empire. But he was forced to put off this retribution, for at that moment he was involved in a major war with Elam, on his southeastern front. He did manage to drive the Elamites back into their own country and was preparing to invade, when still another trouble spot flared up.

This time, Assurbanipal found himself confronting a potential civil war. His brother, Shamash-shum-ukin, had been ruling the city of Babylon for some time, per the dying wish of their father, Esarhaddon. And for seventeen years, Shamash-shum-ukin had not tried to intervene in the affairs of the empire, which Assurbanipal controlled. Eventually, however, Shamash-shum-ukin decided to challenge his brother for the leadership of the empire. Assurbanipal first attempted to alleviate the crisis through diplomacy, but when this approach failed, a civil war did erupt. And after three years of bloody fighting, Shamash-shum-ukin went down to defeat. In an act of despair, he set fire to his own palace and perished in the flames.

Assurbanipal had no sooner restored order to central Mesopotamia when he turned on the Elamites, who had aided his brother in the civil war. This time Elam suffered a fatal dose of Assyrian cruelty. Assurbanipal's troops tore through the heartland of the country, killing, burning, and looting as they went. In a frighteningly short interval, the more than two thousand-year-old Elamite nation was literally erased from the face of the earth.

But in a twist of fate that no one at the time could have foreseen, the victors were about to become the vanquished themselves. Assurbanipal would be the last great king to sit on Assyria's throne. And his sprawling empire, which he and his forefathers were certain would last forever, would soon follow Elam into the waiting jaws of oblivion.

Chapter

4 Society and Life in Ancient Mesopotamia

With occasional exceptions, social organization and everyday life in ancient Mesopotamia were highly tradition-based and homogenous. That is, these aspects of culture were more or less the same among the various peoples who inhabited the area throughout the third, second, and first millennia B.C. The Akkadians, Assyrians, Babylonians, and others borrowed many of their social ideas and customs from the Sumerians, and later on, the Medes and Persians combined various aspects of this traditional Mesopotamian culture with their own Iranian-based traditions.

Modern scholars have not had an easy time piecing together a picture of life in ancient Mesopotamia. The annals of various rulers, some of their personal letters, and a few law codes and legal contracts have survived on tablets found in bas-reliefs, royal archives, and elsewhere. There are also a few writings by Greeks (notably the fifth-century B.C. historian Herodotus) and other foreigners about Mesopotamian customs. Both the native and foreign writings are valuable and useful to be sure. Regrettably, however, most of them deal with the lives of kings, nobles, and other members of the upper classes, who made up a tiny minority of the population. In contrast, references to members of the lower classes in the surviving writings are few and superficial. A traditional Sumerian proverb says, "The poor men are the silent men in Sumer."[40] Although this probably originally referred to the underprivileged having no political power, it could just as well describe the silence about them and their lives in the ancient written records.

To help make up for this silence, historians and archaeologists study physical artifacts. These include the remains of houses, temples, and other buildings, as well as surviving tools and utensils, fragments of pottery, statues and figurines, decayed pieces of furniture, oil lamps, jewelry, grooming items, and so forth. Still, even these finds are often weighted in favor of the wealthy. Only they could afford to build large brick or stone palaces and houses, which because of their size and the quality of their materials have managed partly to withstand the ravages of time. The humble dwellings of the poor, by contrast, along with their meager, perishable belongings, have for the most part deteriorated and disappeared forever.

A King's Image, Duties, and Privileges

Because most of the evidence about Mesopotamian society deals with the upper classes, it is logical to begin with the individual with the highest social status of all—the king. Mesopotamian monarchs generally did not see or portray themselves as gods in human form, as did most Egyptian pharaohs. (There were occasional exceptions; for example, Sargon of Akkad's grandson, Naram-Sin, called himself Din-Gir Naram-Sin, meaning "Naram-Sin the Divine.") Yet these rulers did want to establish a special connection between themselves and the gods to impress both their subjects and their enemies. So official texts and art often used various means to suggest that the kings were divinely chosen, inspired, or guided. According to Stephen Bertman, these means included

references to the king's radiant aura [a halolike light surrounding his person]

Ur-Nammu, king of Ur (left) offers sacrifice to Ur's main god, Sin (seated) in this relief sculpture dating from ca. 2300 B.C.

or to his being the god's "son"; grand epithets, such as "king of the four quarters [of heaven and earth]"; and artistic devices, such as portraying the king standing in a god's presence . . . or making the king taller than the people around him.[41]

This singular relationship with the gods required that the king be the chief god's highest priest as well as the supreme head of state. And it was believed that, for the well-being of the country, the monarch had to be closely guarded and pampered. Physicians and special priests who claimed to be able to interpret divine omens surrounded him at all times, except when he was in his private chambers, and even then they were always within earshot. Also, a staff of court officials and armed guards carefully regulated access to the king and made sure he remained physically safe.

A typical Mesopotamian king had many and diverse duties and responsibilities. First and foremost, he was the supreme commander of the army, with the authority to initiate wars, and some, including many of the Assyrian monarchs, helped map out military campaigns. When holding court, the king appointed governors and other administrators, received and entertained high officials and foreign ambassadors, and dealt with a wide range of appeals and complaints by his subjects. He had the responsibility of seeing that laws were enforced and criminals were punished. In fact, many rulers in the region avidly compiled law codes (Hammurabi being only the most famous) and meted out justice.

As for the king's private life, it goes without saying that he had the largest, most comfortable dwelling in the land. He enjoyed the finest foods, wore elegant clothes, and had hundreds of servants, assistants, and guards to attend to his every need. He also had the luxury of a fully equipped bathroom with a marble toilet that flushed wastes away into drainage holes when servants emptied large jars of water into it. (Only a small handful of rich nobles had such facilities; 99 percent of the population had to relieve themselves in backyards, orchards, and fields.)

NOBLES AND THEIR ESTATES

The relatively small group of nobles under a Mesopotamian king had a somewhat lower social status but enjoyed almost as much privilege and luxury. These individuals included members of the priesthood, high military officers, important dignitaries (such as the palace herald), royal advisers and administrators, provincial governors, district chiefs, and town "mayors." All of these highly placed persons owned large estates, sometimes consisting of dozens or even hundreds of acres, and lived in comfortable houses staffed by many servants.

The manner in which these wealthy estates were acquired reveals much about how traditional Mesopotamian society was structured. Technically speaking, all land in Assyria, Babylonia, and other Mesopotamian states belonged to the king or the religious temples. In practice, however, the ruler and temples granted high-placed persons estates as part of a reward system designed to maintain their continued homage and obedience. Often these holdings

A modern reconstruction of an Assyrian temple. The structure rests in the center of a citadel-like private compound guarded by high walls and battlements.

became hereditary and passed from father to son. Overall, therefore, almost all land in Mesopotamia was part of a royal estate, a temple estate, or a family estate.

The temple estates were controlled and run by prominent priests, who commanded much respect and privilege. By the late third millennium B.C., many of the temples scattered across Mesopotamia had grown into large compounds that included altars, shrines, storehouses, residences, meeting halls, and other structures. The wealth accumulated by such estates and controlled by their priests was the product of a special social-religious relationship they enjoyed with the monarch, who was, of course, looked on as the highest priest

in the land. After a successful war, the monarch turned over a portion of his booty to the temples for their upkeep. He also forced some of the enemies he had captured to work as slaves in the temples.

Still, most of these and the other wealthy estates were not huge, contiguous tracts of land worked by thousands of slaves, like those that developed in Roman Italy several centuries later. The average Mesopotamian estate was relatively moderate in size, covering perhaps 250 acres at most. With the notable exception of the priests on the temple estates, most landlords were absentee, meaning that they lived in a town or city and entrusted the upkeep of their property to a paid manager.

Status and Work in the Lower Classes

The owner and manager of an estate needed agricultural and other kinds of laborers to keep it running, of course. These workers could be freemen, serfs, or slaves depending on the place and time in which they lived, but were often a mixture of all three. (In ancient Mesopotamia, a serf was a person whose social status and legal rights fell somewhere between those of a free laborer and those of a slave.) In addition to those free individuals who hired themselves out as full-time laborers on the big estates, a few apparently owned and worked their own small plots of land. They paid very high property taxes, however, and the government frequently collected these taxes in the form of forced labor rather than money. That meant that, after planting season, many free Mesopotamian peasants had to pay off their tax debts by working for a few months on state building projects (including erecting palaces and digging canals).

The rest of the free workers became craftspeople and professionals of various types. These individuals, who possessed special skills or provided important services, resided mainly in the cities. "The building trades employed architects," Bertman writes, along with,

> brickmakers, stone masons, and carpenters, as well as decorative artists such as sculptors and painters. The food trades were practiced by such workers as fishermen, butchers, bakers, and brewers. Meanwhile, consumer goods were manufactured by bronze workers, silversmiths, goldsmiths, glassmakers, potters . . . leather workers and shoemakers, weavers . . . basketmakers, [and] jewelers. . . . Transportation needs were met by wagonmakers, wagon drivers, shipwrights, and boatmen. In addition, there were street vendors,

A relief from Sennacherib's palace shows prisoners working in a stone quarry.

shopowners, and innkeepers, as well as prostitutes.[42]

By contrast, slaves usually had few skills and almost exclusively performed menial labor. A person became a slave in ancient Mesopotamia in three principal ways, the most common by having the misfortune to be captured in a raid or war. People also bought slaves from slave traders. And at times, free citizens who were seriously in debt sold themselves and/or their families into slavery for as long as it took to work off these debts. A slave was a piece of property, so the law provided for the loss of a slave just as it did the loss of a farm animal or wagon. If a slave "tried to escape," Karen Nemet-Nejat explains,

> he was severely punished. Runaway slaves were rare, but according to one [ancient] text, on their foreheads was marked "A runaway—seize him!" A slave was often distinguished by a characteristic lock of hair, though others wore tags or fetters. The authorities were responsible for capturing runaway slaves and returning them to their masters. The theft of slaves was punished severely, with special laws applied to palace slaves.[43]

Surprisingly, though, Mesopotamian slaves did have a few legal rights, which was unusual in the ancient world. A slave was allowed by law to take part in a business, to borrow money, and to purchase his or her freedom. A slave could also marry, and if he or she married a free person, their children were born as freemen instead of slaves.

HUNTERS AND FARMERS

Whether a nobleman, craftsperson, free laborer, or slave, a Mesopotamian's dwelling and daily routine depended in large degree on where he or she lived. As was true all over the ancient world, the population was broadly divided between country and city dwellers. Most of those who lived in the countryside were either farmers or hunters who worked long hours for few material rewards.

The hunters inhabited the marshlands that grew near the rivers, especially in the well-watered region of southern Mesopotamia near the Persian Gulf. For want of other usable materials, they built their huts from reeds; the marshes had neither large trees nor quarries that supplied wood or stone. To construct such a hut, one tied clusters of tall reeds into thick, sturdy bundles and then dug holes and sank the ends of the bundles into the ground. Next, one bent the bundles over and attached their tops to the tops of other bundles, forming arches. Crosspieces, also made of bundled reeds, connected and braced the arches, after which one tied thick reed mats to the top and sides, forming the hut's roof and walls.

The hunters also made their boats out of marsh weeds. With these small vessels, they caught fish and water fowl, which constituted their main food supply. Usually, a hunter stood upright in his boat. He used a long bamboo pole with a metal tip to spear ducks, heron, and other birds, as well as eels and various kinds of fish.

The other group of rural folk, the farmers and herders, lived in the plains and low foothills. Their houses were usually organized into small villages. The most primitive houses were circular huts made of

This carving from a vase or pitcher shows a farmer pruning a plant.

more permanent homes by using bricks made of clay that had been mixed with straw, stuffed into wooden molds, and dried in the sun. (Bricks that were baked in a kiln were sturdier and lasted longer, but they were more expensive to produce, so generally only the well-to-do could afford them.)

Barley was the most common crop raised by Mesopotamian farmers. The barley kernels could be used whole to make a thick porridge, or they could be ground into flour to make a flat bread that was a staple food throughout the Near East. Another important product made from barley was a tasty, widely popular beer. Many farmers also grew beans, peas, lentils, garlic, cucumbers, lettuce, apples, figs, and grapes.

The oxen the farmers used for plowing were among the domesticated animals bred on farms. Far more numerous, as well as a good deal less expensive to breed and maintain, were the sheep and goats raised by herders. The sheep were crucial to the production of wool for clothes and also an important food source. Small flocks tended by shepherds, often adolescents and even younger children, were an ever-present sight in rural areas.

intertwined branches covered with thatch and loosely cemented with dried mud. The door was made of wood or thatch and hung on a pivot secured to a post driven into the ground or attached to the wall. Some peasants managed to erect slightly

A Guide for Farmers

Following is an excerpt from a document known as the "Farmers' Almanac," a set of instructions designed to guide farmers in proper planting and harvesting, including the use of irrigation channels and dikes. It was discovered at Ur by excavator Charles Leonard Woolley and translated by scholar Samuel Kramer (as quoted in his book *The Sumerians).*

"When you are about to take hold of your field (for cultivation), keep a sharp eye on the opening of the dikes, ditches, and mounds (so that) when you flood the field the water will not rise too high in it. When you have emptied it of water, watch the field's water-soaked ground that it stay virile [fertile] ground for you. Let shod oxen (that is, oxen whose hooves are protected in one way or another) trample it for you; (and) after having its weeds ripped out (by them) (and) the field made level ground, dress it evenly with narrow axes weighing (no more than) two-thirds of a pound each. [Then] let the pickax wielder eradicate [the marks left by] the ox hooves for you (and) smooth them out. . . . When you are about to plow your field, keep your eye on the man who puts in the barley seed. Let him drop the grain uniformly two fingers deep (and) use up one shekel of barley for each *garush*."

LIVING IN THE CITIES

A majority of foodstuffs, wool, and other products that originated in these areas were not used by those who produced them but rather flowed into markets in the cities. Mesopotamia was highly urbanized, so large numbers of city folk had to be fed and clothed. The central sector of such a city featured one or more imposing temples, often perched atop high ziggurats. Around these large-scale buildings stretched an intricate network of residential housing with shops and stables mixed in. "Most homes were entered through narrow alleyways and culs-de-sac," says Nemet-Nejat.

The layout of the narrow streets was like a maze. The street surfaces were uneven, in part due to the constant re-building of homes on previous foundations that were never leveled, and in part because garbage was dumped into the streets. Dogs and other scavenging animals ate some rubbish, but the rest was dried by the sun and walked on.[44]

The typical city house, that of an artisan or laborer, consisted of a modest open-air courtyard with a few small, windowless rooms surrounding it. To ensure privacy and security, all were enclosed by a high wall. Town houses of absentee landlords, government administrators, successful merchants, and other well-to-do individuals had a similar basic layout but were naturally much larger and more comfortable. Such a town house was two stories high and featured a small foyer at ground level in the front. This led into the courtyard, which was paved with kiln-baked bricks and had a drain to keep puddles from forming when it rained. Doors opened off the courtyard to various rooms on the ground floor, including a kitchen, dining area, bathroom, servants' quarters, and a general workroom. On the second floor, accessed by a flight of stairs, was a walkway that ran around the courtyard and led to the family's bedrooms.

The outer wall of such a house afforded the occupants a high degree of visual privacy. However, with so many urban dwellers living in such close-packed conditions, noise must have been a problem. And the crowding, combined

An earthenware model of a small, round-shaped Mesopotamian structure that may be either a shrine or country house fortified to discourage robbers.

with the practice of throwing garbage into the streets, made sanitation an even bigger problem. First, these large populations needed a lot of clean drinking water, as well as water for cooking and cleaning. Most water came from the rivers and the canals fed by them (which is why most cities were built on or very near rivers). Unfiltered river water can carry not only dirt but also a number of germs that cause illness. Some filtering was done by allowing water to sit for a while in stone-lined tanks. The dirt settled out; however, most of the germs surely remained.

One way around this problem was to dig wells, which was the more common approach in Assyria. In Nimrud, for example, several wells reached a depth of ninety feet and provided a large supply of fresh water. (When one of these wells was excavated in 1952, archaeologists were surprised to find that it still gave five thousand gallons of water per day.) An inscription of the Assyrian king Sennacherib describes a windlasslike device used to draw water from the wells in Nineveh: "In order to draw water daily, I had ropes, bronze cables and bronze chains made, and I had beams and crossbars fixed over the wells instead of poles."[45] Sennacherib also constructed an aqueduct, a channel that carries water from its source to a distant city. The channel was about six miles long and made of hardened earth lined with stone.

Despite such efforts, the risk of waterborne illness remained high. Disease

INFESTED BY PESTS

No matter how well built and well kept, nearly all Mesopotamian houses were at one time or another infested by vermin (rats, mice, and so forth) and other creatures, some of which carried disease. This description of Mesopotamian household pests is from Karen Nemet-Nejat's information-packed book *Daily Life in Ancient Mesopotamia.*

"The residences of ancient Mesopotamia housed creeping things such as scorpions; a group of omens referred to scorpions that fell from the ceiling onto a man or his bed. There were even magical and herbal treatments to treat scorpion stings. Snakes also crawled through the house in search of rodents in the branches and mud that formed the roof and ceiling. Here again, omen texts referred to snakes falling out of the roof onto a man or his bed—sometimes this was considered a lucky omen. Even the walls of houses were decorated with different colored species of ants and cockroaches. A number of omen texts indicated the significance to be attached to animals that might be met both inside the house and on its walls—reptiles, lizards, scorpions, cockroaches, beetles, and others."

also spread when germs multiplied in the garbage and other refuse thrown into streets and backyards. In addition, rats and other vermin infested many homes and other structures; and some of these creatures carried fleas that themselves carried disease germs, including those that cause the deadly bubonic plague. Thus, periodic small-scale epidemics were a fact of city life.

No one yet knew of the existence of germs, of course, so it was assumed that disease was a punishment inflicted by angry gods. The average Mesopotamian doctor was a combination of magician and faith healer, therefore. He used various spells and chants designed to drive away the demons of illness or appease the angry gods. (A few doctors were more practical and prescribed herbs, ointments, and simple kinds of surgery in addition to the usual magic spells.)

This tiny figurine depicts a woman of the town of Lagash holding a vase. In general, women were second-class citizens.

MARRIAGE AND WOMEN'S ROLES

Despite living in such crowded conditions in which sanitation was difficult and illness common, city dwellers, both rich and poor, were proud and protective of their homes and families. As remains true today, marriage was seen as the fundamental basis for raising a family. However, among the Sumerians and Babylonians (and likely the Assyrians, too), marriage was less about love and more about perpetuating tradition and civic order. The main goal was to have children who would carry on the old ways and dutifully maintain an orderly and efficient society. Not surprisingly then, a marriage was in many ways a business arrangement, and

Buying a Wife at Auction

The Greek historian Herodotus, who visited Mesopotamia in the mid-fifth century B.C., reported in his now-famous *Histories* that in addition to arranged marriages, in earlier centuries local men sometimes chose their wives in public auctions.

"In every village, once a year all the girls of marriageable age used to be collected together in one place, while the men stood around them in a circle; an auctioneer then called each one in turn to stand up and offered her for sale, beginning with the best-looking and going on to the second-best as soon as the first had been sold for a good price. Marriage was the object of the transaction. The rich men who wanted wives bid against each other for the prettiest girls, while the humbler folk . . . were actually paid to take the uglier ones. . . . The money came from the sale of the beauties, who in this way provided dowries for their ugly or misshapen sisters. It was legal for a man to marry his daughter to anyone he happened to fancy. . . . In cases of disagreement between husband and wife, the law allowed the return of the purchase money. . . . This admirable practice has now fallen into disuse."

to be binding, it required a legal contract. Law number 128 in Hammurabi's code reads: "If a man takes a wife and does not arrange a contract for her, that woman is not a wife."[46] Thus, says Bertman, every marriage began

> with a negotiation between the representatives of two families: between the prospective groom and his prospective father-in-law, or between the father of the prospective groom and the father of the bride-to-be. . . . It was the family that was paramount rather than the individual. . . . Indeed, before the wedding . . . the bride and groom might not have known each other personally.[47]

Once married, the wife had to defer to her husband in most matters, since Mesopotamian society was decidedly male dominated. It is possible that women in poor farm households shared equally in the decision making with their husbands. In general, however, women were second-class citizens who were fairly tightly regulated by their husbands and fathers. In some legal ways, women were equal to men; women could own land, for example, and sue in court, even for divorce. But men controlled financial affairs, and a wife had to get her husband's permission to take part in any sort of business transaction. Only if he died and she had no son to take over the household could she assume control of the finances and run the house.

Marriage was generally monogamous, with one wife to a husband, except under certain special conditions. When a wife could not bear children, for instance, a husband was allowed either to take a second wife or to have children with a female servant. Nevertheless, he remained legally bound to continue honoring and supporting his wife. And the servant could not claim equality with the wife. Hammurabi's law number 146 provides that if the servant "bears children and afterwards claims equal rank with her mistress," the wife "may not sell her," but "may reduce her to bondage and count her among the slaves."[48]

However, if a woman committed adultery or some other offense, the law was no longer on her side. One of Hammurabi's laws states that "if the wife of a man is caught lying with another man, they [the authorities] shall bind them and throw them into the water." Another statute in the same code says that "if she . . . has gadded about, neglecting her house and belittling her husband, they shall throw that woman into the water."[49] It is unlikely that all such infractions led to the extreme penalty of drowning. More often, the woman probably received a beating or some other physical punishment, which was permitted in Mesopotamian society. An Assyrian law, discovered in the early twentieth century in the ruins of the city of Assur, reads: "Apart from the penalties for a married woman . . . a man may flog his wife, he may pull out her hair, he may damage and split her ears. There is nothing wrong in this."[50] It is possible that such spousal abuse was more common in Assyria than in other parts of Mesopotamia, but evidence of how widespread it actually was or how often it occurred is lacking.

The evidence is also sparse regarding women's roles outside the home. However, it is known that a few young women, mainly from wealthy homes, became priestesses. Also, some women became "factory" workers. Such factories were state-run workrooms in which small or large groups of people wove carpets, embroidered clothes, made jewelry, or produced other goods for use by the well-to-do classes. Records found at Ur describe one factory that had eight separate departments, including ones for carpenters, goldsmiths, and leather workers. Some evidence suggests that many workers in these establishments were women, some of them free and others slaves. Women also worked as wine sellers, as shown by this law from Hammurabi's code: "If bad characters gather in the house of a wine seller and she does not arrest those bad characters and bring them to the palace, that wine seller shall be put to death."[51] In addition, as in all societies, women worked as prostitutes.

The treatment of women as second-class citizens, their subservience to men, and the exploitation of women's labor and bodies are revealing of the nature of Mesopotamian society. In many ways it was unique to its time and place. Yet it featured some elements quite common to later cultures, both in the East and West and including many in modern times.

5 Mesopotamia Under the Medes and Persians

Considering the many centuries of energy, toil, and blood that had gone into the making of the mighty Assyrian Empire, its unmaking was surprisingly sudden, catastrophic, and permanent. The exact reasons for Assyria's fall are unclear. This is because the same year that King Assurbanipal utterly destroyed the kingdom of Elam—639 B.C.—royal record keeping in Assyria abruptly halted. So the final twelve years of that monarch's reign must be pieced together from scattered foreign sources. These suggest that Assyria was suddenly engulfed by a combination of invasions, rebellions, and civil strife on a huge scale. This makes sense. For a long time, the Assyrians had conquered and looted their neighbors, while managing to hold together their far-flung empire by brute force. Assyria therefore made numerous bitter enemies and at the same time fatally overextended itself.

The Assyrian kings also did not pay proper attention to ominous developments in the mountainous lands north and east of the Persian Gulf. They viewed the Medes and other inhabitants of that region as backward folk who posed little threat to Mesopotamia as a whole. This assessment turned out to be mistaken, however. The Medes slowly but steadily built a formidable kingdom with an effective army that eventually marched westward and, with the help of the Babylonians, overran the Assyrian heartland. This significantly altered the geopolitical map of the Near East. Yet that map soon underwent another drastic change, as a subject people of the Medes, the Persians, became the next great empire builders in the region.

RISE OF NEO-BABYLONIA AND MEDIA

Though little is known about the events immediately following the fateful year of 639 B.C., it appears certain that Assyria was wracked by civil strife. Following Assurbanipal's death in 627, two of his sons—Assur-etil-ilani and Sin-shar-ishkun—battled each other and Assur-etil-ilani won. Perhaps he was killed in a new round of civil disorders, for only four years later he was gone and Sin-shar-ishkun was king.

At the same time that these royal brothers fought each other, their nation faced steadily mounting external threats. All over the Near East, its subjects and vassals took advantage of its troubles, either severing ties with the central authority in Nineveh or simply ignoring it.

The biggest of these threats came from Assyria's longtime nemesis, Babylonia. In 626 B.C. a Chaldean prince named Nabopolassar killed or chased away the Assyrian troops occupying Babylon and seized control of the city. This marked the beginning of the most renowned of Babylonia's royal dynasties, the Chaldean, also called the Neo-Babylonian, which would hold sway in southern Mesopotamia for almost a century.

Nabopolassar was not content simply to rule Babylon. Gathering his forces, he rapidly drove the Assyrians out of Babylonia and back into their own heartland. He even laid siege to the city of Assur, although he failed to take it. Still, the Assyrians were so disorganized and desperate that at this point they swallowed their pride and asked for the help of a subject people they had treated particularly cruelly—the Egyptians. Probably because they feared the rising power of Babylonia more than the now declining power of Assyria, the Egyptians agreed to send aid.

However, the Egyptian troops did not reach troubled Assyria in time. This was partly because Babylonia suddenly found a powerful ally whose intervention significantly speeded up the disintegration and collapse of the Assyrian realm. That ally—the Medes—had originated in the highlands of western Iran perhaps around 1000 B.C. At first, they were little more than a loose confederation of tribes, but they steadily grew more populous and powerful during the same years that the Assyrians were seizing large sectors of the Near East. Beginning in the eighth century B.C., the Assyrians and Medes clashed from time to time, as shown in the inscriptions of Assyrian kings such as Tiglathpileser III and Sargon II. But various treaties were signed, and in any case, Media lay far from the central authority in Nineveh and remained largely independent of Assyrian control. So the Medes continued to gain strength.

Eventually, circa 625 B.C., an unusually dynamic and ambitious ruler ascended the

BABYLONIA'S ATTACK ON ASSYRIA

This surviving Babylonian chronicle quoted in Daniel Luckenbill's *Ancient Records of Assyria and Babylonia* describes King Nabopolassar's 616 B.C. assault on Assyria's heartland.

"In the tenth year [of his reign], Nabopolassar, in the month of *Aiaru* [April/May], mobilized the Babylonian army and marched up the bank of the Euphrates. . . . In the month of *Abu* [July/August] they reported that the Assyrian army was in the city of Kablini. Nabopolassar went up against them. . . . He made an attack upon the Assyrian army. The army of Assyria . . . sustained a decisive defeat. They took many of them prisoners . . . and [many of] the nobles of Assyria they captured."

An Assyrian relief sculpture shows Medes bringing tribute to King Sargon II. Boots with upturned toes were common among the Medes and Persians.

Median throne. He was Cyaxares II. According to the Greek historian Herodotus, Cyaxares instituted a major program of military expansion and reorganization. The new king divided his spearmen, archers, and cavalry into distinct units, each of which was trained separately and used in a specific manner on the battlefield. He also instituted standardized military uniforms that would thereafter become a trademark of Median and Persian soldiers. (These outfits consisted of a long-sleeved leather tunic that ended above the knee, leather trousers, laced shoes with projecting tips, and a round felt cap with a neck flap.) Many of Cyaxares' troops were native Medes. But he also called on recruits from minor Iranian peoples who had become Median vassals, among them the Persians.

Assyria's Collapse

With his strong new army, Cyaxares decided it was time for his kingdom to enter the looming power struggle in Mesopotamia. In 615 B.C., less than a year after Nabopolassar and his Babylonians had begun to drive back the Assyrians, Cyaxares' forces suddenly entered Assyria and assaulted Assur. According to a Babylonian chronicle, the Median king "descended the Tigris, encamped against Assur, made an assault upon the city and captured it. The city he destroyed. He inflicted a bad defeat on the people and nobles."[52] Learning of this event, Nabopolassar hurried his own army to the scene. Although he arrived too late to share in the victory and spoils, both he and Cyaxares realized that an alliance against their mutual foe would be advantageous.

Faced with this formidable coalition of enemies, the Assyrian realm, already badly weakened and disorganized, buckled and collapsed. In the summer of 612 B.C., the Babylonian and Median forces swept into the Assyrian heartland north of Assur, taking town after town. Finally, the invaders reached and sacked Assyria's largest and most important city—Nineveh. News of the city's destruction quickly spread far and wide, eventually reaching faraway Judah, in Palestine. There, the prophet Nahum wrote this vivid sketch of the chaos and bloodshed attending what was then seen as a momentous event:

> The shatterer [Cyaxares? Nabopolassar? The hand of God?] has come up against you [the Assyrians]. Man the ramparts . . . collect all your strength. . . . The shield of his mighty men is red, his soldiers are clothed in scarlet. The chariots flash like flame when mustered in array; the chargers prance. The chariots rage in the streets, they rush to and fro through the squares; they gleam like torches, they dart like lightning. . . . The river gates are opened, the palace is in dismay; its mistress [the queen?] is stripped, she is carried off, her maidens lamenting. . . . Nineveh is like a pool whose waters run away. "Halt! Halt!" they cry; but none turns back. Plunder the silver, plunder the gold! There is no end of treasure, or wealth of every precious thing. Desolate! Desolation and ruin! Hearts faint and knees tremble, anguish is on all loins, all faces grow pale![53]

It appears that a few diehard Assyrian nobles and their followers escaped this devastation and held out for a while somewhere on the upper reaches of the Euphrates. The Babylonian-Median assault continued, however. And after 610 B.C., the Assyrian throne and government simply ceased to exist. Meanwhile, Assyria's heartland, which had remained continuously inhabited and prosperous for almost two thousand years, lay devastated. All that remained of the Assyrian Empire was the memory of its cruelty.

Rise of Cyrus the Persian

With the once-powerful Assyria eliminated from the scene, Neo-Babylonia and Media were the chief powers in

Mesopotamia. Cyaxares had favorably positioned his kingdom to acquire and long maintain a large empire in the region. However, his successor, Astyages, failed to fulfill this great promise. Astyages was a self-indulgent, ineffective ruler who spent most of his time enjoying the pomp and ceremony of the newly sumptuous Median court at Ecbatana, the Median capital. Both the Median nobles and the kingdom's subject peoples rapidly grew discontented with their new king. And that made Media potentially vulnerable to any ambitious opponent who might dare to make a power play.

Just such an opponent soon materialized in the person of a local Persian noble named Cyrus. Born in the small Persian homeland of Fars, on the northeastern shore of the Persian Gulf, he grew up during an era when that homeland was a vassal state of Media. When he became ruler of Fars in 558 B.C., at the age of about forty-one, he was not content with what he viewed as Persian servitude to

THE BATTLEMENTS OF ECBATANA

The unification of the Median tribes into a nation was primarily accomplished by two local kings—Deioces (ca. 700–647 B.C.) and his son Phraortes (ca. 647–625 B.C.). In this excerpt from his *Histories*, the Greek historian Herodotus described how Deioces built an impressive new capital city.

"Deioces' first act was to command his subjects to build a palace worthy of a king, and to grant him the protection of a private guard. The Medes complied; they built a large and well-defended palace on a site he himself indicated, and allowed him to select a bodyguard without restriction of choice. Once firmly on the throne, Deioces put pressure on the Medes to build a single great city to which, as the capital of the country, all other towns were to be held of secondary importance. Again they complied, and the city now known as Ecbatana was built, a place of great size and strength fortified by concentric walls, these so planned that each successive circle was higher than the one below it by the height of the battlements. . . . The circles are seven in number, and the innermost contains the royal palace and treasury. . . . The battlements of the five outer rings are painted in different colors, the first white, the second black, the third crimson, the fourth blue, the fifth orange; the battlements of the two inner rings are plated with silver and gold respectively. These fortifications were to protect the king and his palace; the people had to build their houses outside the circuit of the walls."

These floors and broken columns are all that remains of Cyrus's once magnificent palace at Pasargadae, in present-day Iran.

Media. Seeing that Astyages was a weak king, Cyrus led a rebellion against the Medes and about the year 550 B.C. managed to capture Ecbatana. According to Herodotus, a few of Astyages's soldiers remained loyal to him,

> but of the remainder, some deserted to the Persians and the greater number deliberately . . . took to their heels. When Astyages learned of the disgraceful collapse of the Median

army, he swore that even so Cyrus should not get away with it so easily. . . . He armed all Medes, both under and over military age, who had been left in the city, led them out to battle and was defeated. His men were killed and he himself was taken alive.[54]

Although he had handily defeated Media, Cyrus did not destroy it or its rich culture. Demonstrating the wisdom and leniency of a great ruler, he actually embraced Median culture. For example, he gave many Median nobles high positions in his court and generalships in his army and transformed the Median homeland into the first province, or satrapy (a Median word borrowed by the Persians), of his own empire. Cyrus also made Ecbatana his second capital, after his own capital of Pasargadae in the hills of Fars. In these ways, Cyrus created for himself an image of a strong but fair and civil ruler, and as a result, most of his subjects, including the defeated Medes, greatly admired him.

CYRUS'S MILITARY REFORMS

Being ambitious as well as just, Cyrus desired to push the empire's boundaries beyond those Cyaxares had established. (Already the realm encompassed most of the former Assyrian homeland, Syria, and much of western Iran.) But to pursue this goal, he needed a strong and flexible military system. And he spent the rest of his life diligently developing and perfecting an army that became feared throughout the Near East and well beyond.

In large degree, Cyrus modeled his army on that of the Assyrians, although he modified and improved their system. First, he increased the depth of the average battlefield formation of archer-pairs, which created a heavier concentration of arrows shot. He also developed an elite corps of mounted warriors drawn from the Persian nobility. And he ordered significant improvements in the construction of chariots, making them more destructive when used in direct frontal assaults on enemy lines. "He had chariots of war constructed with strong wheels," the fourth-century B.C. Greek historian Xenophon wrote in his account of Cyrus's life,

> so that they might not easily be broken, and with long axles; for anything broad is less likely to be overturned. The box for the driver he constructed out of strong timbers in the form of a turret; and this rose in height to the driver's elbows, so that they could manage the horses by reaching over the top of the box; and besides, he covered the drivers with mail [armor], all except their eyes. On both sides of the wheels, moreover, he attached to the axles steel scythes [blades] . . . with the intention of hurling the chariots into the midst of the enemy.[55]

To supplement these regular army units, as well as act as his personal bodyguards, Cyrus created an elite group of soldiers. He called them the Amrtaka, or "Immortals," a reference to the fact that if one died, he was immediately replaced. Both commoners and nobles served in the Immortals, as well as in the infantry, cavalry, and chariot corps. Military service was compulsory for all Persian men between the ages of twenty and twenty-four and some stayed in the service until they were as old as fifty.

THE CONQUESTS OF CYRUS

When Cyrus was satisfied that his new military machine was up to the task, he initiated a series of conquests. At the

The defeated king of Lydia, Croesus, stands before the victorious Cyrus. The former Lydian kingdom became a satrapy (province) of Persia.

time, the Persian realm was one of four great powers that held sway in the Near East. The other three were Babylonia, Egypt, and Lydia (which roughly encompassed the heartland of the old Hittite Empire in Asia Minor). Cyrus attacked Lydia first, leading his troops into Asia Minor in 546 B.C.

Taken unawares by this bold move, the Lydian king, Croesus, was in a quandary. So he decided to follow a custom of the Greeks, whom he greatly admired, and consulted the famous oracle at Delphi, a town in the central region of mainland Greece. (The oracle was a priestess who was thought to be a medium between the gods and humans.) The oracle declared that if Croesus crossed the Halys River, in central Asia Minor, and attacked the Persians, he would destroy a great empire. Filled with confidence, the Lydian king led his troops across the Halys and attacked. But soon it became clear that he had misinterpreted the prophecy, for the empire that was destroyed turned out to be his own. Cyrus drove the Lydians back to their capital of Sardis (located about fifty miles inland from the Aegean coast), captured the city, and began to transform Lydia into another Persian satrapy. (As part of this process, the Persians demanded and received tribute from the Greek cities on Asia Minor's western coast; this marked the first direct contact between Greeks and people from Mesopotamia and Iran.)

Cyrus's defeat of Lydia upset the balance of power in Mesopotamia and the rest of the Near East. The Babylonians, whose realm occupied the central and southern portion of Mesopotamia, were naturally worried. And that worry turned to trepidation as they watched the Persians

go on to conquer most of the lands north and east of the Persian Gulf in only a year or two. The Babylonian king, Nabonidus, was certain that his kingdom would be Cyrus's next target. And sure enough, in 539 B.C. the Persian king invaded Babylonia. Nabonidus's army was no match for the battle-hardened Persian forces, and it did not take long for the city of Babylon to fall. On October 29, Cyrus made a triumphant entry into the city and in his first official proclamation stated: "I am Cyrus, king of the universe, Great King, mighty king, king of Babylon, king of Sumer and Akkad, king of the world quarters."[56]

In this way, Cyrus was able to add Babylonia's territories to his growing empire. These lands included all of southern Mesopotamia and most of Palestine. The only major Near Eastern power left at this point was Egypt, and Cyrus began the huge task of preparing to invade that country. He did not live to see these plans come to fruition, however; for in about 530 B.C., while campaigning in the east near the Aral Sea, he died shortly after suffering a battle wound. His officers bore his body back to Pasargadae and placed it in a simple but beautiful stone tomb, which survives to this day as a monument to one of the most ambitious and talented rulers in history.

ASCENDANCY OF CAMBYSES AND DARIUS

Fortunately for Cyrus, his empire did not fall apart after his passing, as had happened with Cyaxares and the Median realm. Cyrus's immediate successors, his son, Cambyses II, and an even more successful monarch, Darius I, continued to

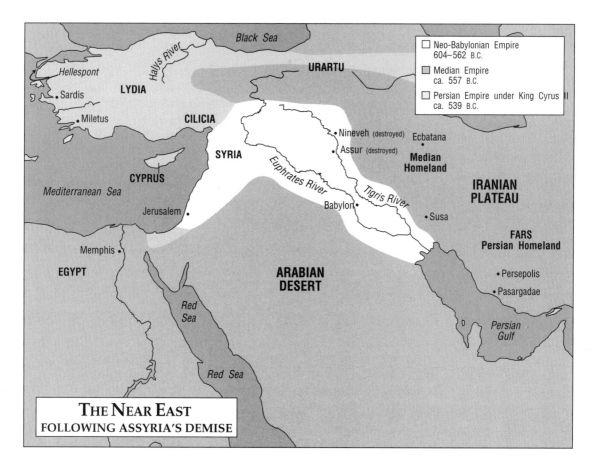

THE NEAR EAST
FOLLOWING ASSYRIA'S DEMISE

expand the empire, making it the largest the world had yet witnessed. On his father's death, Cambyses continued the preparations for the Egyptian campaign. This included the construction of Persia's first fleet of ships. Persia's rapid transformation from a mere land power to master of both sea and land widened the scope of its potential future conquests.

Early in 525 B.C., Cambyses led his massive land and naval forces through Palestine and into Egypt. Near Pelusium, on the seacoast just east of the Nile Delta, the pharaoh Psammetichos (or Psamatik) III and his own troops met the invaders but were quickly defeated. The young

pharaoh fled for his life, and the rest of the country fell to the Persians without any further large-scale battles.

Cambyses remained in Egypt for the next three years to consolidate his gains and then headed for home. He had only just begun his long journey when he received news that a man named Gaumata had led an insurrection in Ecbatana and usurped Persia's throne. Gaumata claimed to be Cambyses's brother, Bardiya, to whom the impostor bore an uncanny physical resemblance. The problem was that Cambyses had earlier secretly murdered the real Bardiya, so most Persians assumed that Gaumata was whom he claimed to be.

DARIUS'S GREAT CLIFF SCULPTURE

In this excerpt from his informational *Handbook to Life in Ancient Mesopotamia,* Stephen Bertman describes Darius's famous carvings at Behistun.

"On the royal road between Babylon and Ecbatana stands a 1,700-foot-high cliff. Around 520 B.C., the Persian king Darius I ordered a monument to be carved on its sheer face celebrating his triumph over insurgents. On a sculpted relief, he stands with his foot on a prostrate enemy as defeated chieftains cower before him, their hands tied behind their backs, their necks connected by rope. Accompanying the relief is an immense cuneiform inscription totaling 1,200 lines and measuring about 100 feet high by 150 feet wide. To make the rock face more durable, the entire surface was highly polished by the Persians and then thickly varnished."

Cambyses was anxious to reach the capital and depose the imposter. But Cambyses died (perhaps of an infection after cutting himself with a knife) before he could make it. Gaumata continued to hold on to power for about seven more months (March to September 522 B.C.), after which a small group of leading Persian nobles assassinated him. They installed one of their own number, Darius, on the throne.

Like Cyrus and Cambyses before him, Darius desired to expand the realm. But first the new king had to deal with a flurry of rebellions that had broken out when news had spread of the false Bardiya's death. "The governors of the distant provinces," historian Percy Sykes writes, "thinking possibly that the empire of Persia would share the fate of Media, desired to carve out kingdoms for themselves. Darius, therefore, had to conquer, and in some cases to reconquer, the many kingdoms of which the empire consisted."[57]

Babylonia was only one of these provinces that Darius brought back into the Persian fold as he crushed the revolts one by one.

Having regained control of his empire, Darius delivered a stern warning to any future would-be rebels by making a gruesome example of a Median noble who had dared to rebel. The unfortunate man suffered the loss of his nose, ears, tongue, and eyes, after which he was impaled and hanged, still living, for all to see on Ecbatana's royal gate. In another display of naked power, Darius celebrated his victories over the rebels by ordering the creation of a huge (ten by eighteen feet) stone carving on the face of a cliff at Behistun, southwest of Ecbatana. The sculpture, which has survived, shows the king standing triumphant before nine subservient rebel leaders, all bound at their necks by a single rope. Meanwhile, Darius's left foot rests on the belly of a prostrate rebel leader, who vainly pleads for mercy.

DARIUS'S REFORMS

Darius had learned a valuable lesson from the rebellions, namely, that in the past the provincial governors had been allowed to accumulate too much local power, and that posed an ever-present threat to the central authority. So he reorganized the empire by dividing it into twenty satrapies, giving the governor of each satrapy only certain administrative powers. The military authority that a governor used to wield was given instead to a general who reported directly to the king. In addition, Darius assigned special royal inspectors who visited and spied on the satrapies on a regular basis to make sure that no treasonous activities were taking place.

Another way that Darius bound his distant provinces more securely to the central authority was to institute important improvements in long-distance communications. He created a large-scale system of roads, which allowed his royal couriers and also his armies to move swiftly from one section of the realm to another. These roads, which were surfaced with hard-packed earth and well maintained, also made the movement of commercial goods easier and faster. Several roads branched out from Babylon. But the most renowned of Darius's royal roads stretched over fifteen hundred miles from Susa, near the head of the Persian Gulf, to Sardis, near the shore of the Aegean Sea. "At intervals all along the road are recognized

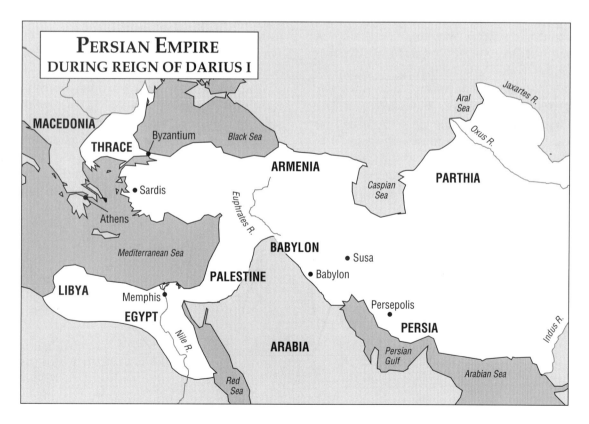

PERSIAN EMPIRE
DURING REIGN OF DARIUS I

stations, with excellent inns," wrote Herodotus, who actually traveled on this road.

> The road itself is safe to travel by, as it never leaves inhabited country. In Lydia and Phrygia [in central Asia Minor], over a distance of . . . about 330 miles—there are 20 stations . . . . The total number of stations, or post-houses, on the road from Sardis to Susa is 111. . . . Traveling at the rate of 150 furlongs [18 miles] a day, a man will take just ninety days to make the journey.[58]

In contrast, Darius's royal couriers were able to cover this great distance in only fifteen days. To accomplish this feat, which at the time was seen as almost superhuman, the riders changed mounts at each road station and took small naps in the saddle, much like the Pony Express riders in the American West.

Darius's many reforms and domestic projects (which also included building impressive canals and palaces) kept him busy. Evidence suggests that he frequently traveled among the major cities of the region, including Susa and Babylon, to keep a close eye on developments. But he also invested considerable time and effort in military development and new conquests. Before his time, most Persian troops were natives levied from the provinces, including Babylonia, the former Assyria and Elam, and other areas of the Near East. Darius started a practice that his successors would follow—a major use of paid foreign mercenaries to supplement the regular soldiers. Thereafter, a typical Persian army was a motley mixture of soldiers from many lands, each contingent bearing its own native variety of armor and weapons.

Darius kept many of these troops well occupied as he engaged in new conquests. These expeditions probed lands lying far from the heart of the Persian realm, centered in southern Mesopotamia and Fars. In 519 B.C., for instance, a Persian army subdued the Saka, a people who inhabited the remote, rugged region northwest of India. Later, on his western flank, Darius decided to conquer the Scythians, who inhabited the region west of the Black Sea. This particular foray, though fairly unremarkable in and of itself, was to have major historical consequences. It was the first invasion of European soil by a Mesopotamian-based realm, and it would soon lead to the first major clashes between Western and Near Eastern armies.

Chapter

6 East Meets West: The Greeks in Mesopotamia

When Darius, king of Persia, crossed what is now the Bosporus Strait and entered Europe in 512 B.C., he initiated the first major contact between Western and Eastern civilizations. His immediate target was Scythia, the forested, culturally backward region lying west and northwest of the Black Sea. (The Scythians were a seminomadic tribal people who made their living mainly by raising cattle and other livestock. They had no cities, writing system, or formal government comparable to those of the Persians and Greeks.) Darius was no doubt partially drawn to the area by rumors of abundant gold. But there is little doubt that he was also thinking about eventual expansion much deeper into Europe. At the same time that he marched on Scythia, he sent out ships carrying scouts; they first mapped the Greek coasts and then continued on to southern Italy. The scouts' reports must have described huge tracts of land filled with natural resources that were ripe for Persian picking.

Standing in the way of these grandiose dreams of extending Near Eastern rule into Europe were the tiny city-states of mainland Greece and the nearby Greek islands. Darius was already familiar with some Greeks because the Greek cities of western Asia Minor (a region then called Ionia) were already part of his empire. His predecessor, Cyrus, had easily conquered the Ionian Greeks, who had since that time not given the Persians any significant trouble. So Darius likely viewed all Greeks as a docile and rather insignificant people dwelling on the edge of the civilized world (the center of that world, in his view, being Mesopotamia and southern Iran). Surely, he reasoned, they would not pose an impediment to his imperial goals in Europe.

But Darius was dead wrong. The Greeks, both on the Greek mainland and in Ionia, ended up giving him much more trouble than he had bargained for. The Greek states twice stood up to and defeated the Persian colossus, forever halting its advance into Europe. Moreover, these victories filled the Greeks with confidence and inspired them to greater goals. Eventually, led by the young Macedonian king Alexander III, later called "the Great," they turned the tables on and invaded Persia. All of Mesopotamia, along with other parts of the Near East, fell under Greek control, and the area received its first major infusion of Western ideas and customs.

Persia's King Darius I holds audience in his palace at Persepolis. Darius made the mistake of assuming that the Greeks would be easy to defeat.

"REMEMBER THE ATHENIANS"

The series of events leading to the Greek eclipse of Mesopotamia began with Darius's invasion of Scythia, which proved largely a failure. The natives wisely avoided getting involved in formal pitched battles with the Persians; instead, the Scythians burned their own crops so the invaders could not use them and continually retreated into the wilderness. The expedition was far from a waste of time, however. After leaving Scythia, Darius conquered Thrace, the region lying directly north of the Aegean Sea, and transformed it into a

new satrapy, which he named Skudra. This gave Persia a firm foothold in Europe to be exploited later.

Darius was forced to return to the area sooner rather than later, however. In 498 B.C. the Ionian Greeks, who had long dreamed of regaining their freedom, rebelled against Persia. Aristagoras, a distinguished citizen of Miletus, the most prosperous Ionian city, instigated the insurrection and managed to secure aid from two mainland Greek city-states, Athens and Eretria. Darius's local officials were forced to flee inland to the provincial capital of Sardis. And the revolt soon spread northward into Thrace, where the inhabitants of that region also threw off the Persian yoke. A contingent of Ionians and Athenians even had the gall to attack and burn Sardis.

A proud man who had a reputation for crushing rebellions, Darius responded by vowing to put down the revolt and then punish the upstart Athenians and Eretrians. According to Herodotus, the indignant Persian king

asked who the Athenians were, and then, on being told, called for his bow. He took it, set an arrow on the string, shot it up into the air and cried: "Grant, O God, that I may punish the Athenians." Then he commanded one of his servants to repeat to him the words, "Master, remember the Athenians," three times, whenever he sat down to dinner.[59]

The next four years witnessed Darius fulfilling the first part of his vow with a vengeance. His troops subdued the Ionian cities, many of which were put to the torch; large numbers of captured Greek children were dragged back to Mesopotamia, where the boys became servants and the girls entered Darius's harem. Then the king sent his son-in-law, Mardonius, to reconquer Thrace. Once this goal was accomplished, it was time to punish Athens and Eretria. For this task, Darius chose his nephew, Artaphernes, and a capable Median general named Datis. With a force of perhaps twenty-five thousand soldiers and twice that many sailors and other supporters, they crossed the Aegean in the summer of 490 B.C., landed on the eastern shore of the Greek mainland, and sacked Eretria.

Datis and Artaphernes were confident in the impending success of their second objective—the destruction of

THE PERSIANS BESIEGE MILETUS

The Persians learned about siege tactics from the Assyrians. In 494 B.C., as King Darius put down the Ionian revolt, the large and prosperous Greek city of Miletus fell after his forces besieged it. In this excerpt from his *Histories*, Herodotus briefly described the siege and its outcome.

"[The Persians] invested Miletus by land and sea. They dug saps [tunnels] under the walls, brought up rams of all kinds, and, five years after the revolt of Aristagoras, overwhelmed it. So Miletus was reduced to slavery. . . . Most of the [Milesian] men were killed by the Persians . . . the women and children were made slaves, and . . . the men in the city whose lives were spared were sent as prisoners to Susa; Darius did them no harm, and settled them in Ampe, on the Persian Gulf, near the mouth of the Tigris."

Athens. But when they landed at Marathon, about twenty-five miles northeast of Athens, the city's entire citizen-militia of some nine thousand soldiers was waiting for them. The Greek troops were more heavily armored than the Persians. They also fought in a special formation called a phalanx. It had a depth of eight ranks, or rows, of fighters whose uplifted shields formed a formidable unbroken protective barrier. As this formation marched toward an enemy, the men in the front rank jabbed their spears at their opponents, while the hoplites in the rear ranks pushed at their comrades' backs, giving the whole unit a tremendous and lethal forward momentum. These advantages paid off at Marathon, as the Persians went down to defeat, losing at least 6,400 men. (Only 192 Athenians were killed.)

Xerxes Invades Greece

When the news of the outcome at Marathon reached Darius, he grew angrier than ever at the Greeks, whom he saw as impudent upstarts. "He was more than ever determined to make war on Greece," Herodotus wrote.

> Without loss of time he dispatched couriers to the various states under his dominion with orders to raise an army much larger than before; and also warships, transports, horses, and grain. So the royal command went round; and all Asia was in an uproar for three years, with the best men being enrolled in the army for the invasion of Greece.[60]

It was not Darius who ended up leading this great expedition, however. He died in 486 B.C. and his son, Xerxes (ZERK-seez), took his place on the throne. After more war preparations and various delays, early in 480 B.C. the new king marched westward at the head of the largest invasion force assembled anywhere in the world in ancient times. It consisted of an estimated 200,000 combat infantry and cavalry; 800 to 1,000 ships manned by at least 150,000 oarsmen and sailors; and a huge following of support personnel and camp followers numbering perhaps as many as 300,000.[61] Many of these troops were drawn from Babylonia, Assyria, and other parts of Mesopotamia.

This huge force seemed unstoppable, even to many Greeks. Yet incredibly, the Greeks did stop it. Although each city-state was able to field only a few hundred men, and in some cases a few thousand at most, many of these states stood together against the invaders. At the pass of Thermopylae, about a hundred miles northwest of Athens, Xerxes defeated and wiped out a tiny force of Greeks. But it was a hollow victory, for the defenders, led by Sparta's King Leonidas, had bravely held back the Persians for days and killed close to twenty thousand of them.

Another hollow victory was Xerxes' capture of Athens, which occurred on or about September 17, 480 B.C. The Persians found the city largely deserted. And while they were setting it afire, the Athenians and other Greeks were preparing to meet the invaders in a great sea battle. Near the island of Salamis, a few miles southwest of Athens, the allied Greek fleet decisively defeated Xerxes' own larger fleet. And the following summer, the Greeks annihilated

Eyewitness to a Persian Defeat

The Persian defeat at Salamis in 480 B.C. was a pivotal turning point because it spelled the end of Persia's ambitions for conquest in Europe. This excerpt from *The Persians* (Philip Vellacott's translation) by the Athenian playwright Aeschylus, who fought in the battle, is a partial eyewitness account. The lines are spoken by a Persian messenger who has returned to Susa and describes the disaster to the queen mother.

"At once ship into ship battered its brazen beak. A Greek ship charged first, and chopped off the whole stern of a Persian galley. Then charge followed charge on every side. At first by its huge impetus our fleet withstood them. But soon, in that narrow space, our ships were jammed in hundreds; none could help another. They rammed each other with their prows of bronze; and some were stripped of every oar. Meanwhile the enemy came round us in a ring and charged. Our vessels heeled over; the sea was hidden, carpeted with wrecks and dead men; all the shores and reefs were full of dead. Then every ship we had broke rank and rowed for life. The Greeks seized fragments of wrecks and broken oars and hacked and stabbed at our men swimming in the sea. . . . The whole sea was one din of shrieks and dying groans, till night and darkness hid the scene."

most of the Persian land army near Plataea, north of Athens. Still another Greek victory occurred only a few days later at Mycale, on the Ionian coast.

Greek Troops in the Near East

In light of these wholly unexpected and stunning events, Xerxes had to abandon his plans for conquering Greece and Europe. Perhaps he viewed his losses as an unfortunate but temporary setback in the "inevitable" Persian conquest of the known world. If so, he was mistaken. Time would prove the Persian failure in Greece a prelude to the fall of Meso-potamia and most of the rest of the Near East to Greek armies.

In the years following the Persian retreat from Greece, Athens organized over 150 city-states from the Greek mainland, Aegean Islands, and Ionia into the Delian League. The primary objective of this powerful political-military alliance was to defend Greece against further Persian incursions. But the league soon went on the offensive as well. It attacked the coasts of Asia Minor, forcing Xerxes to send one

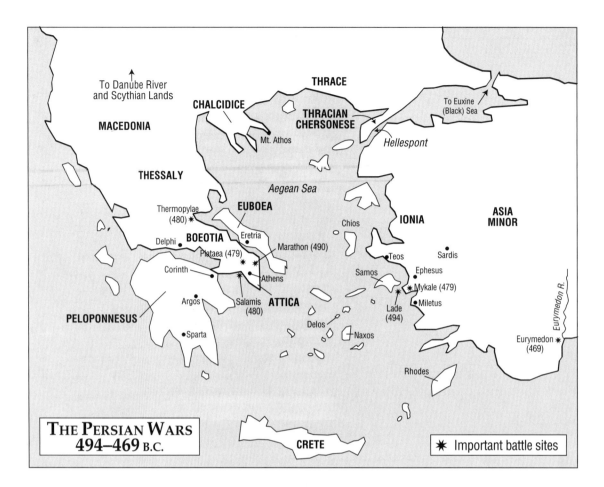

**THE PERSIAN WARS
494–469 B.C.**

To Danube River
and Scythian Lands

THRACE

CHALCIDICE

THRACIAN
CHERSONESE

To Euxine
(Black) Sea

MACEDONIA

Mt. Athos

Hellespont

THESSALY

Aegean Sea

ASIA
MINOR

Thermopylae
(480)

EUBOEA

Chios

IONIA

Delphi

BOEOTIA

Eretria

Marathon (490)

Sardis

Plataea (479)

Teos

Ephesus

Corinth

Samos

Mykale (479)

Athens

Miletus

Argos

Salamis
(480)

ATTICA

Lade
(494)

PELOPONNESUS

Delos

Eurymedon R.

Sparta

Naxos

Eurymedon
(469)

Rhodes

CRETE

✳ Important battle sites

army after another into the area. And later, Xerxes' successor, Artaxerxes, endured a major setback when a large force of Athenians aided the Egyptians in a large-scale rebellion against the Persians.

Even more telling was a series of events that occurred during the reign of a later Persian king, Artaxerxes II. The young monarch's brother, Cyrus (whom the Greeks called "Cyrus the Younger" to differentiate him from the first Persian king of that name), launched a rebellion in a bid to seize the throne. Cyrus raised a large army consisting of about a hundred thousand Persians and some ten thousand Greek mercenaries.

The great showdown took place in the heart of Mesopotamia in 401 B.C. Cyrus led his army toward the Euphrates, hoping his brother would back down and avoid a battle. But at Cunaxa, about fifty miles from Babylon, the king had assembled an army even bigger than Cyrus's. As the fight commenced, the Greek phalanx charged the enemy with devastating effect. But by the end of the day, Cyrus was dead and his native troops completely defeated.

That left the small Greek army surrounded by hostile forces in the middle of the Mesopotamian plains. Soon the Greek commanders were lured to a peace conference, where the Persians treacherously murdered them. The Greeks then elected new leaders, among them the historian Xenophon, who later described the plight he and his companions faced. The Greeks, he said, "were distant from Greece more than a thousand miles, with no guide for the road. Impassable rivers crossed the homeward way, and they had been deserted even by the natives who had come up country with Cyrus."[62] Incredibly, the Greeks managed to overcome these obstacles. And after successfully fighting their way across Mesopotamia, they made it to the Black Sea and Greek-controlled territory.

This now-famous "March of the Ten Thousand" proved a crucial turning point for the future of the cities and people of Mesopotamia. It had demonstrated to Greeks everywhere that even in the center of the Persian realm, Persian troops were no match for Greek troops. This was a lesson that later Greek generals would take to heart.

The Fall of Persia

One of these Greek generals was Philip II, king of Macedonia, a kingdom in northern Greece. Before his time, Macedonia had been disunited, militarily weak, and culturally backward. But after he ascended the

throne in 359 B.C., he swiftly transformed the country into a strong, unified state with a powerful standing army. In 338 B.C. Philip, assisted by his teenaged son Alexander, defeated a group of Greek city-states that had united against him.

No sooner had Philip become "captain-general" of a new Macedonian-controlled Greece than he began preparing for a large-scale invasion of Persia. (His publicly announced motive was revenge for the Persian invasions of Greece a century and a half before. But his real reasons were personal ambition and a strong belief in the superiority of Greek culture.) Philip did not lead the fateful expedition, however. He was assassinated in 336 B.C., leaving his young son as Macedonia's king and Greece's supreme commander.

A modern cameo purports to depict Philip II as a young man.

Alexander was eager to carry on the crusade against Persia. In 334 B.C., when he was only twenty-two, he marched an army numbering 32,000 infantry and 5,000 cavalry into Asia Minor. His first victory came at the Granicus River, where he defeated a large Persian force. Next, he engaged the reigning Persian king, Darius III, at Issus, in Syria. Victorious once more, Alexander marched southward through Palestine and liberated Egypt from Persian domination.

Finally, in 331 B.C., Alexander turned toward Mesopotamia, no doubt with Xenophon's account of the March of the Ten Thousand fresh in his mind. The Greek invasion force now numbered about 40,000 infantry and 7,000 cavalry. Alexander reached the former Assyrian heartland in September 331 B.C. And on October 1, at Gaugamela, a few miles southeast of the ruins of Nineveh, Darius met him with a force of about 100,000 soldiers, 200 war chariots, and 15 battle elephants. According to the first-century A.D. Greek writer Plutarch in his biography of Alexander:

> With shouts of encouragement, to one another, the [Greek] cavalry charged the enemy at full speed and the phalanx

Alexander's army defeats that of Darius III, elephants and all, at Gaugamela (also called Arbela) in October 331 B.C.

rolled forward like a flood. Before the leading ranks could engage, the barbarians [i.e., the Persians] began to fall back, hotly pursued by Alexander, who drove the retreating enemy towards the center, where Darius was stationed.

As Alexander and his horsemen made this bold thrust into the enemy lines, Plutarch continued, Darius's bodyguards panicked

at the terrible sight of Alexander bearing down upon them and driving the fugitives before him. . . . As for Darius, all the horrors of the battle were now before his eyes. The forces which had been stationed in the center for his protection had now been driven back upon him. It had become difficult to turn his chariot around and drive it away, since the wheels were encumbered and entangled with heaps of bodies. . . . In this extremity, the king abandoned his chariot and his armor, mounted a mare . . . and rode away.[63]

When Darius's troops heard that he had fled, most of them did the same, leaving Alexander and the Greeks to celebrate an enormous victory.

Alexander chased after Darius for several months. Finally, in June 330 B.C., a Persian governor named Bessus betrayed and captured the king. Bessus illegally declared himself the royal successor, and soon afterward he and his supporters stabbed Darius with their spears and left him in a wagon on the roadside. Less than an hour later, one of Alexander's soldiers found the dying man and gave him water. According to this soldier, the last words of the Persian Empire's last king were,

This is the final stroke of misfortune, that I should accept a service from you, and not be able to return it, but Alexander will reward you for your kindness, and the gods will repay him for his courtesy towards my mother and my wife and my children [whom Alexander had already captured and was treating with kindness and respect]. And so, through you, I give him my hand.[64]

(Alexander eventually caught up with Bessus and ordered first that he have his nose and ears cut off, according to Persian custom, and second that he be executed.)

THE FATE OF ALEXANDER'S EMPIRE

In contrast with the Greek troops who had followed Cyrus the Younger seven decades before, the Greeks fighting for Alexander did not have to retreat from Mesopotamia. After more campaigns in the east (which took them to the borders of India), Alexander's men followed him back to Babylon. At his urging, many of them took Persian brides; some of these Greeks settled down to work and raise families on lands once inhabited by Sumerians, Akkadians, Assyrians, Amorites, and many others.

Meanwhile, Alexander wanted to make Babylon the capital of his world empire. (He now controlled all of the former Persian realm, plus Greece, and had plans to

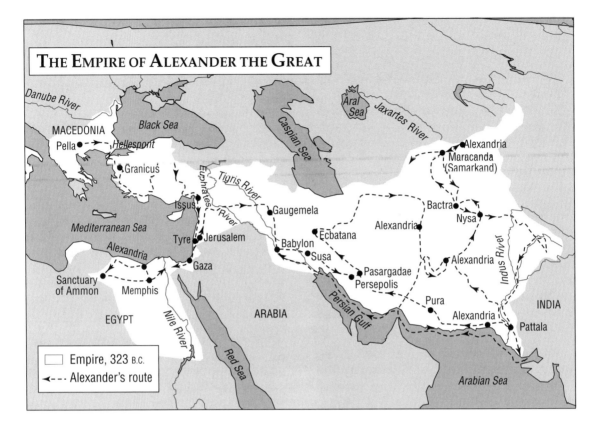

THE EMPIRE OF ALEXANDER THE GREAT

Danube River

MACEDONIA
Pella
Hellespont
Black Sea
Granicus
Aral Sea
Jaxartes River
Caspian Sea
Euphrates River
Tigris River
Issus
Mediterranean Sea
Gaugemela
Alexandria
Maracanda (Samarkand)
Bactra
Nysa
Tyre
Jerusalem
Ecbatana
Alexandria
Alexandria
Babylon
Susa
Gaza
Pasargadae
Persepolis
Indus River
Sanctuary of Ammon
Memphis
ARABIA
Persian Gulf
Pura
Alexandria
INDIA
EGYPT
Nile River
Red Sea
Arabian Sea
Pattala

□ Empire, 323 B.C.

◄--- Alexander's route

turn westward and conquer the rest of Europe.) Before he could realize this and his other ambitious goals, however, he died in Babylon, possibly of malaria, in 323 B.C. He was only thirty-three.

Because Alexander had died so suddenly and so young, his empire was not destined to fill the vacuum left by Persia's collapse. Instead, control over Mesopotamia and the rest of the Near East now fell to other Greeks. First, Alexander's leading generals and governors, who came to be called the Diadochoi, or "Successors," faced off and for the next forty-odd years waged almost unrelenting war. Among the most powerful and successful of these men were Antigonus the "One-Eyed," the first of the Successors to take the title of king; his colorful but brutal son, Demetrius; and two shrewd and ambitious men—Ptolemy (TAW-luh-mee) and Seleucus.

MESOPOTAMIA UNDER THE SELEUCIDS

Ptolemy managed to gain control over Egypt, where he founded the Greek Ptolemaic dynasty. But by the early third century B.C., most of the rest of the Near East, including Mesopotamia, became the dominion of Seleucus. Modern historians call the Seleucid Empire and other Greek realms that emerged from the Successor wars Hellenistic, meaning "Greeklike," because their societies often featured various Near Eastern languages, customs, and ideas overlaid by a veneer of Greek ones.

Indeed, in Seleucid-controlled Mesopotamia, Greek culture became the model to follow, particularly among the upper classes. Many bureaucrats, army officers, and traders migrated into the region from mainland Greece. And Seleucus built several new cities that were physically and culturally patterned after Greek ones. One of these, Seleucia-on-the-Tigris, slightly northeast of Babylon, became his capital and a major focal point of trade routes passing through Mesopotamia. This new city steadily drew both population and business away from Babylon, which went into decline. Nevertheless, Mesopotamia as a whole remained as prosperous as it had ever been. According to Michael Grant:

> The role of Mesopotamia as a source of commercial revenue for the [Seleucid] kings was specially important. . . . Under [them] it became extremely productive once again. Its great potential fertility was exploited by efficient irrigation, its . . . industry flourished, and trading and banking reached a high degree of development. . . . Much of this prosperity was due to Seleucia-on-the-Tigris. . . . [It] was a river port for maritime shipping, linked with settlements on the Persian Gulf . . . where vessels from southern

THE SELEUCID TYCOONS

In this excerpt from his book *From Alexander to Cleopatra: The Hellenistic World*, scholar Michael Grant explains how trade was the lifeblood of the Seleucid rulers of Mesopotamia, who became extremely wealthy.

"Although agriculture was important to the Seleucids, it was not as important as international trade, which they elevated to unprecedented dimensions. Every Seleucid king was a tycoon on an enormous scale, making millions from the great trade routes from the Mediterranean to central Asia, India, and Arabia, routes which passed through their empire and were served by a network of good roads. Trading was also facilitated by the creation of an impressive unified coinage, which the rulers issued themselves and made the basic currency of the whole of their huge territories, speeding up the process, begun by the Persians, of transforming an economy of kind [bartered goods] onto a monetary basis. Even if, therefore, they were occasionally hard pressed by the ambitious dimensions of their policies, the Seleucid kings remained immensely rich."

Arabia and India called on their way up the Tigris. But Seleucia was also the center upon which all the main land-routes converged. . . . Few places have ever so effectively dominated the business affairs of half a continent.[65]

On the negative side, this great prosperity was not felt at all levels of society. The reality was that it became increasingly difficult for non-Greeks to get ahead in Mesopotamia. As Greek culture continued to permeate the region, there emerged a classist society no less unfair than the ones that had preceded it. Now, though, it was not so much differences in wealth that divided the classes as much as differences in ethnicity, most important the difference between Greeks and non-Greeks. Greeks clearly enjoyed higher social status and privilege than native Mesopotamians. As Chester Starr puts it: "Groups of relatively few Greeks constituted an upper crust [in society] much as did the English masters of Bombay, Singapore, or Hong Kong in the nineteenth century."[66]

Under these conditions, Greek naturally became an important language in the region, one essential to government circles. Yet other languages, notably Aramaic and cuneiform Akkadian, remained prominent, especially in regions where fewer Greeks settled. Also, Seleucus and his heirs recognized the importance of maintaining other facets of old Mesopotamian culture to make ruling this large and ancient land easier; after all, the reasoning went, too much change might be too jarring and stir up unrest. So they kept most of the old Persian bureaucratic structure and dutifully supported and perpetuated the traditional temples and worship of the Babylonians and other native peoples. An example is revealed by the following inscription, carved by Seleucus's son, Antiochus I, onto the temple of Nabu (the Assyrian and Babylonian god of the written word, as well as son of the chief Babylonian god Marduk). In structure and tone, it is little different from the traditional religious inscriptions of the region.

> Antiochus, the great king . . . king of the world, king of Babylon . . . the first son of Seleucus, the king . . . of Babylon, am I. . . . In the month of Addaru, on the twentieth day, year 43 [i.e., the forty-third year since Seleucus established his empire], the foundation of Ezida, the true temple, the house of Nabu, which is in [the town of] Borsippa, I did lay. O Nabu, lofty son [of Marduk], wise one of the gods . . . regard [me] joyfully and, at your lofty command which is unchanging, may the overthrow of the countries of my enemies . . . just kingship, [and] a happy reign . . . be [your] gift for the kingship of Antiochus . . . forever.[67]

FROM CRADLE TO GRAVE

These efforts to create a workable balance between Greek and traditional Mesopotamian cultures was well-meaning and in some areas of the realm successful. However, the Seleucids' great political and cultural experiment was never completed because their empire was very short-lived. In fact, less than a century after it was founded, the realm was in serious decline.

First, the Seleucid rulers frequently warred with other Hellenistic realms, which drained precious human and material resources. Second, in 238 B.C. a group of nomadic Iranian tribesmen seized most of the old Persian satrapy of Parthia (southeast of the Caspian Sea). Their leader, Arsaces, established the Parthian dynasty, whose aggressive rulers steadily chipped away at the Seleucid realm. Another major setback

A bust of the Seleucid ruler Antiochus III, who was defeated by Rome.

occurred in 190 B.C., when the Romans, masters of the Italian peninsula, disastrously defeated the Seleucid ruler Antiochus III, killing more than fifty thousand of his troops.

For these and other reasons, the Seleucid Empire continued to decline. And by 141 B.C. most of it, including Mesopotamia, had been completely absorbed by the Parthian Empire. (A few more Seleucid rulers held out in Syria until 63 B.C., when Rome finally annexed the area.) The departure of the Greek rulers and their supporters did not mean that all Greeks and their influence were gone. Thousands of Greek farmers and artisans remained in Mesopotamia, and Seleucia-on-the-Tigris and some other predominantly Greek cities continued to prosper.

However, the Seleucid Greek interlude had marked an important turning point in Mesopotamia. The Seleucid government was the last strongly centralized administration that both based itself in and tried to maintain the full economic potential of the fertile Mesopotamian plains. Increasingly less of that potential would be realized in the centuries to come. And eventually, much of the region would dry out and become sparsely populated. Once the cradle of civilization, for the distant descendants of Sargon, Hammurabi, and Cyrus, it would become almost a grave.

Mesopotamia in Later Ages

After the fall of the Persian and Greek dynasties in Mesopotamia, the fertility and prosperity of the region began to decline, fairly slowly at first, but eventually with increasing rapidity. As a whole, the Parthian Empire, which replaced the Seleucid realm in the second century B.C., prospered for more than three centuries. In large degree this was because the Parthians were the middlemen in the valuable "silk route" that carried luxury goods from faraway China to the Mediterranean world. The industriousness of the remaining Greeks in the region also contributed to prosperity. Parthian rulers wisely tolerated a number of Greek customs and allowed a few all-Greek cities, notably Seleucia-on-the-Tigris, a fair amount of autonomy. The wealth generated by these cities partially benefited these rulers.

In what ultimately proved counterproductive to prosperity, however, the Parthians introduced a kind of feudalism. In this system, strong vassal lords ruled the provinces like tiny kingdoms. They swore a higher allegiance and paid monetary tribute to an overall king, who ruled from Ctesiphon, a Parthian city erected alongside Seleucia-on-the-Tigris. But these local lords largely controlled the resources and economies of their respective territories. Some were productive rulers, but many were not. And under the less productive ones, sections of Mesopotamia, including the crucial irrigation canals, suffered neglect.

THE SĀSĀNIAN DYNASTY

Partly because of Parthia's lack of a strong centralized administration, over time its rulers grew weaker and less able to maintain the allegiance of their vassals. Finally, in A.D. 224, the last Parthian king, Artabanus V, was overthrown by Ardashîr, a popular local leader from the old Persian stronghold of Fars. Ardashîr established the Sāsānian dynasty (named for one of his ancestors, Sāsānian), which remained in power for the next four centuries.

Unfortunately for Mesopotamia, during these centuries its plains became the scene of numerous wars and battles among Sāsānians, Romans, and many others. One result of these conflicts was that a number of towns were destroyed and never rebuilt. Also, the Sāsānian rulers' strong central imperial administration (which replaced the less centralized Parthian system) concentrated most of its attention on the needs of the

Ahura-Mazda and another god bestow kingship on the Sāsānian ruler Ardashir.

Iranian provinces and tended to neglect the Tigris and Euphrates river valleys. So as time went on, many of Mesopotamia's once-fertile fields dried out and a number of the ancient towns that had escaped ruin in the wars was abandoned.

Thus, the passage of many centuries—aided by wars, conquests, frequent changes of culture and language, and widespread poverty and neglect—took an awful toll on Mesopotamia. The glories of Sumer and Akkad, of Assyria and Babylonia, and of Cyrus's Persia and Seleucus's Greek empire became distant memories. As Stephen Bertman puts it, with the sudden and violent end of the Sāsānians in the seventh century, "the history of ancient Mesopotamia ends."[68]

The Ziggurat and crumbling walls of once mighty Ur stand in mute testimony to the former greatness of Mesopotamian civilization.

Arabs, Mongols, Turks, and Iraqis

That violent end of the Sāsānian Empire came at the hands of an Arab army, part of a zealous burst of Islamic conquests that rocked and forever changed the Near East. In 634 the forces of a strong Muslim Arab leader, Umar I, swept out of the Arabian peninsula into Palestine and southern Mesopotamia. In 637 these forces crushed the army of the last Sāsānian king, Yazdegerd III, at Kadisiya, near the old Parthian capital of Ctesiphon. Yazdegerd fled from one province to another until he was finally assassinated in 651, marking the end of the Sāsānian dynasty.

The Arabs ruled Mesopotamia until 1258, when an Asian people, the Mongols, conquered parts of the Near East. Following the Arabs and Mongols, a number of other outside peoples took possession of the region, which remained only marginally prosperous in comparison with the glory days of its ancient empires. In 1432 Turkish tribes wrested control of Meso-potamia from the Mongols; in 1508 the Ottoman Turks achieved dominance in the region; and in 1918, at the close of World War I, the British supplanted the Ottomans.

In a sense, the modern history of Mesopotamia began in 1932, when much of its ancient territory was incorporated into the new independent nation of Iraq. By this time, large sections of the region were parched desert wastes. But a new source of wealth—abundant underground supplies of oil—began to be exploited. Unfortunately, however, as in the past, only a minority of the people benefited from this prosperity. Foreign companies and local dictators got rich while most Iraqis remained poor. Moreover, throughout the remainder of the twentieth century, the region witnessed many violent changes of government, wars, and other turmoil; the latest episode was in 2003, when the U.S. military deposed the regime of the hated Iraqi dictator Saddam Hussein. Americans and many Iraqis hope that democracy, a system the region has never known, will take hold on the plains where long ago the world's first cities rose. If this new dream is realized, Mesopotamia may enjoy a well-deserved renaissance, and its people will prosper once more.

Notes

Introduction: Who Were the First Mesopotamians?

1. Chester G. Starr, *A History of the Ancient World.* New York: Oxford University Press, 1991, p. 18.

2. Starr, *A History of the Ancient World*, pp. 18–19.

3. Michael Grant, *The Ancient Mediterranean.* New York: Penguin, 1969, p. 20.

4. Samuel N. Kramer, *Cradle of Civilization.* New York: Time, 1967, p. 16.

5. William Ryan and Walter Pitman, *Noah's Flood: The New Scientific Discoveries About the Event That Changed History.* New York: Simon and Schuster, 1998, pp. 234–36.

6. H.W.F. Saggs, *Babylonians.* Berkeley: University of California Press, 2000, p. 22.

Chapter 1: The First Cities, Empires, and Literature

7. Karen R. Nemet-Nejat, *Daily Life in Ancient Mesopotamia.* Peabody, MA: Hendrickson, 1998, p. 14.

8. Gwendolyn Leick, *The Babylonians.* London: Routledge, 2003, p. 26.

9. H.W.F. Saggs, *Civilization Before Greece and Rome.* New Haven: Yale University Press, 1989, p. 45.

10. Michael Wood, *Legacy: The Search for Ancient Cultures.* New York: Sterling, 1992, p. 25.

11. Saggs, *Babylonians*, p. 70.

12. Saggs, *Babylonians*, p. 71.

13. Stephen Bertman, *Handbook to Life in Ancient Meso-potamia*, New York: Facts On File, 2003, p. 266.

14. Kramer, *Cradle of Civilization*, pp. 39–40.

15. Quoted in Joan Oates, *Babylon.* London: Thames and Hudson, 1986, p. 52.

Chapter 2: Rise of the Assyrians and Babylonians

16. Leick, *Babylonians*, p. 33.

17. Quoted in Jorgen Laessoe, *People of Ancient Assyria: Their Inscriptions and Correspondence*, trans. F.S. Leigh-Browne. London: Routledge and Kegan Paul, 1963, p. 43.

18. Quoted in Daniel D. Luckenbill, ed., *Ancient Records of Assyria and Babylonia*. 1926. vols. Reprint, New York: Greenwood Press, 1968, vol. 1, p. 17.

19. Quoted in Laessoe, *People of Ancient Assyria*, p. 76.

20. Kramer, *Cradle of Civilization*, p. 52.

21. Quoted in Saggs, *Babylonians*, p. 103.

22. Quoted in Saggs, *Babylonians*, p. 104.

23. Quoted in James B. Pritchard, ed., *Ancient Near Eastern Texts Relating to the Old Testament.* Princeton: Princeton University Press, 1969, p. 178.

24. Quoted in Trevor Bryce, *The Kingdom of the Hittites.* Oxford: Clarendon Press, 1998, p. 103.

25. Bryce, *Kingdom of the Hittites*, p. 104.

26. Leick, *Babylonians*, p. 47.

27. Trevor Watkins, "The Beginnings of Warfare," in John Hackett, *Warfare in the Ancient World*, New York: Facts On File, 1989, p. 28.

28. Quoted in Luckenbill, *Ancient Records*, vol. 1, p. 51.

Chapter 3: The Assyrian Empire Reaches Its Zenith

29. Nahum 3:2–3, in Bible.

30. Quoted in Luckenbill, *Ancient Records*, vol. 1, pp. 110, 111.

31. Quoted in Luckenbill, *Ancient Records*, vol. 2, pp. 74–75.

32. Quoted in Luckenbill, *Ancient Records*, vol. 2, p. 45.

33. Quoted in Luckenbill, *Ancient Records*, vol. 2, p. 152.

34. Second Chronicles 32:10–13, in Bible.

35. Quoted in Luckenbill, *Ancient Records*, vol. 2, p. 183.

36. Starr, *A History of the Ancient Records*, p. 135.

37. Quoted in Luckenbill, *Ancient Records*, vol. 2, p. 244.

38. Quoted in Luckenbill, *Ancient Records*, vol. 2, p. 227.

39. Quoted in Luckenbill, *Ancient Records*, vol. 2, p. 293.

Chapter 4: Society and Life in Ancient Mesopotamia

40. Quoted in Kramer, *Cradle of Civilization*, p. 127.

41. Bertman, *Handbook to Life in Ancient Meso-potamia*, p. 66.

42. Bertman, *Handbook to Life in Ancient Meso-potamia*, p. 248.

43. Nemet-Nejat, *Daily Life in Ancient Mesopotamia*, p. 118.

44. Nemet-Nejat, *Daily Life in Ancient Mesopotamia*, pp. 103–4.

45. Quoted in Nemet-Nejat, *Daily Life in Ancient Mesopotamia*, p. 111.

46. Quoted in Robert F. Harper, trans., *The Law Code of Hammurabi*. Chicago: University of Chicago Press, 1904, p. 57.

47. Bertman, *Handbook to Life in Ancient Meso-potamia*, p. 276.

48. Quoted in Harper, *Law Code of Hammurabi*, p. 58.

49. Quoted in Harper, *Law Code of Hammurabi*, p. 59.

50. Quoted in Saggs, *Civilization Before Greece and Rome*, p. 169.

51. Quoted in Harper, *Law Code of Hammurabi*, p. 32.

Chapter 5: Mesopotamia Under the Medes and Persians

52. Quoted in Luckenbill, *Ancient Records*, vol. 2, pp. 418–19.

53. Nahum 2:1–10, in Bible.

54. Herodotus, *The Histories*, trans. Aubrey de Selincourt. New York: Penguin, 1972, p. 95.

55. Xenophon, *Cyropaedia*, trans. Walter Miller. New York: Macmillan, 1914, vol. 2, pp. 135–37.

56. Quoted in A.T. Olmstead, *History of the Persian Empire*. Chicago: University of Chicago Press, 1948, p. 51.

57. Sir Percy Sykes, *A History of Persia*. 1915. Reprint, London: Macmillan, 1958, vol. 1, p. 160.

58. Herodotus, *Histories*, pp. 369–70.

Chapter 6: East Meets West: The Greeks in Mesopotamia

59. Herodotus, *Histories*, p. 382.

60. Herodotus, *Histories*, p. 441.

61. These estimates are by modern historians and military experts. Herodotus's figures, including 1.75 million infantry, 100,000 mounted troops, 510,000 sailors, and more than 2 million camp personnel, are hugely exaggerated, for such a gigantic host could not have sustained itself on the march.

62. Xenophon, *Anabasis*, published as *The March Up Country*, trans. W.H.D. Rouse. New York: New American Library, 1959, p. 66.

63. Plutarch, *Life of Alexander*, in *Plutarch: The Age of Alexander*, trans. Ian Scott-Kilvert. New York: Penguin Books, 1973, pp. 290–91.

64. Quoted in Plutarch, *Life of Alexander*, p. 300.

65. Michael Grant, *From Alexander to Cleopatra: The Hellenistic World*. New York: Charles Scribner's Sons, 1982, pp. 59–60.

66. Starr, *A History of the Ancient World*, p. 408.

67. Quoted in Pritchard, *Ancient Near Eastern Texts*, p. 317.

Epilogue: Mesopotamia in Later Ages

68. Bertman, *Handbook to Life in Ancient Mesopotamia*, p. 58.

For Further Reading

Books

David Ali et al., *Great Civilizations of the East*. London: Southwater, 2001. A big, handsomely illustrated book that examines the rise of various Asian cultures, including those of ancient Mesopotamia.

Dale Brown, ed., *Mesopotamia: The Mighty Kings*. New York: Time-Life, 1995. This attractively illustrated book with many color photos and drawings deals mainly with the better-known Assyrian and Babylonian rulers.

Michael W. Davison, ed., *Everyday Life Through the Ages*. London: Reader's Digest, 1992. This large, beautifully illustrated volume, which examines the way people lived in various cultures throughout history, has sections on ancient Assyria, Babylonia, and Persia.

Samuel N. Kramer, *Cradle of Civilization*. New York: Time, 1967. Written by one of the world's foremost scholars of Mesopotamian culture and lavishly illustrated with stunning photos and drawings, this remains one of the best basic presentations of Mesopotamian civilization for general readers.

Harold Lamb, *Cyrus the Great*. Garden City, NY: Doubleday, 1960. Though old, this modern telling of the life and times of Cyrus, founder of the Persian Empire, is not dated. Its straightforward style makes it readily accessible to junior high school readers.

Carol Moss, *Science in Ancient Mesopotamia*. London: Orchard, 1999. An easy-to-read introduction to mathematics and other science-related endeavors in ancient Mesopotamia.

Tim Wood, *Ancient Wonders*. New York: Penguin Books, 1991. This beautifully illustrated and informative volume examines the most famous buildings and monuments of ancient times, including the Hanging Gardens of Babylon, built by the son of the Babylonian ruler who destroyed the Assyrian Empire.

Websites

The Babylonians, Croft-Crossland's Standard World History (http://home.cfl.rr.com). Though brief, this synopsis of ancient Babylonia is well written and includes some striking photos of surviving artifacts.

Persia, the International History Project (http://ragz-international.com). A brief but informative overview of Persian history, with numerous links to related topics.

The Sumerians, Croft-Crossland's Standard World History (http://home.cfl.rr.com). An excellent general overview of the Sumerians, including a useful map of early Mesopotamia and many stunning color photos.

Major Works Consulted

Modern Sources

Stephen Bertman, *Handbook to Life in Ancient Mesopotamia.* New York: Facts On File, 2003. University of Windsor scholar Stephen Bertman has compiled a tremendous resource about this topic, including pertinent information about geography, government, law, religion, writing and literature, architecture, the arts, trade, weapons and warfare, food, clothing, education, and much more. Very highly recommended.

Jean Bottero, *Everyday Life in Ancient Mesopotamia.* Baltimore: Johns Hopkins University Press, 2001. A noted scholar examines living conditions in the ancient Mesopotamian empires.

Andrew R. Burn, *Persia and the Greeks: The Defense of the West, c. 546–478 B.C.* London: Edward Arnold, 1962. This masterful scholarly work covers the rise of Persia under Cyrus the Great in the sixth century B.C., his conquest of the Greek Ionian cities, and the Persian invasions of Greece under Darius's general, Datis, and later, Darius's son, Xerxes. Well written and carefully documented.

John Curtis, *Ancient Persia.* Cambridge, MA: Harvard University Press, 1990. A short but informative volume summarizing Persian history, ethnicity, art, and architecture.

Michael Grant, *From Alexander to Cleopatra: The Hellenistic World.* New York: Charles Scribner's Sons, 1982. An excellent general overview of the Hellenistic age, this volume contains a useful sketch of the Greek Seleucid dynasty that ruled Mesopotamia after the fall of Persia.

Peter Green, *Alexander of Macedon, 356–323 B.C.: A Historical Biography.* Berkeley: University of California Press, 1991. One of the best modern studies of Alexander, this detailed, well-researched volume by a widely respected historian contains much valuable information about the Persian Empire during its decline in the fourth century B.C.

———, *The Greco-Persian Wars.* Berkeley: University of California Press, 1996. Another fine volume by Green, this is a detailed, heavily documented, up-to-date overview of relations between the Persians and Greeks, including excellent descriptions of the various military campaigns and engagements.

Samuel N. Kramer, *The Sumerians: Their History, Culture and Character.* Chicago: University of Chicago Press, 1971. An invaluable source of information about early Mesopotamia, including a great deal of primary source material, clearly written by one of the great twentieth-century experts in the field. Highly recommended.

Gwendolyn Leick, *The Babylonians.* London: Routledge, 2003. An intelligent, fact-filled study of ancient Babylonian history and culture.

Karen R. Nemet-Nejat, *Daily Life in Ancient Mesopotamia.* Peabody, MA: Hendrickson, 1998. The author begins with an impressive and useful historical overview (although she does not include the Persian and Seleucid periods of Mesopotamia), then covers nearly all aspects of everyday life in a thorough manner.

A.T. Olmstead, *History of the Persian Empire.* Chicago: University of Chicago Press, 1948. A huge work that covers, often in intricate detail, nearly all aspects of ancient Persian history, ethnicity, customs, government, military methods, art, architecture, and religion. The writing is rather dry and ponderous, however, so it will appeal mainly to scholars and those with a strong interest in ancient Mesopotamia.

A. Leo Oppenheim, *Ancient Mesopotamia: Portrait of a Dead Civilization.* Chicago: University of Chicago Press, 1977. A highly detailed, well-written, and informative discussion of Mesopotamian culture by one of the recognized masters in the field.

Susan Pollock, *Ancient Mesopotamia.* New York: Cambridge University Press, 1999. A well-written survey of ancient Mesopotamian history and culture.

Georges Roux, *Ancient Iraq.* New York: Penguin, 1980. An extremely comprehensive and well-written overview of Mesopotamian history and culture, from the prehistoric period through the rise and fall of the major peoples who dominated the region—the Sumerians, Akkadians, Babylonians, Assyrians, Persians, Seleucid Greeks, and Parthians. Highly recommended for serious students of the subject.

H.W.F. Saggs, *Babylonians.* Berkeley: University of California Press, 2000. Saggs, of University College, Cardiff, here delivers a very readable overview of the ancient Babylonians. He traces their roots in the rise of Mesopotamian cities and pre-Babylonian empires and ends with a discussion of Babylon in the Bible and classical literature. Highly recommended.

———, *Civilization Before Greece and Rome.* New Haven: Yale University Press, 1989. One of the best recent books summarizing the cultural contributions of the early Near Eastern civilizations.

Daniel C. Snell, *Life in the Ancient Near East, 3100–332 B.C.* New Haven: Yale University Press, 1997. This sweeping overview of Near Eastern culture, customs, and ideas by Professor Snell, of the University of Oklahoma, is up-to-date, briskly written, informative, and copiously documented. Highly recommended.

Ancient Sources in Translation

Aeschylus, *The Persians*, in *Aeschylus: Prometheus Bound, The Suppliants, Seven Against Thebes, The Persians.* Trans. Philip Vellacott. Baltimore: Penguin, 1961.

Arrian, *Anabasis Alexandri*, published as *The Campaigns of Alexander*. Trans. Aubrey de Selincourt. New York: Penguin Books, 1971.

C.W. Ceram, ed., *Hands on the Past: Pioneer Archaeologists Tell Their Own Story*. New York: Knopf, 1966.

Stephanie Dalley, trans., *Myths from Mesopotamia*. New York: Oxford University Press, 1989.

Benjamin R. Foster, ed., *From Distant Days: Myths, Tales, and Poetry of Ancient Mesopotamia*. Bethesda, MD: CDL Press, 1995.

Norma L. Goodrich, *Ancient Myths*. New York: New American Library, 1960.

Robert F. Harper, trans., *The Law Code of Hammurabi*. Chicago: University of Chicago Press, 1904.

Herodotus, *The Histories*. Trans. Aubrey de Selincourt. New York: Penguin, 1972.

Jorgen Laessoe, *People of Ancient Assyria: Their Inscriptions and Correspondence*. Trans. F.S. Leigh-Browne. London: Routledge and Kegan Paul, 1963.

Austen Henry Layard, *Nineveh and Its Remains*. 2 vols. London: John Murray, 1867.

Daniel D. Luckenbill, ed., *Ancient Records of Assyria and Babylonia*. 1926. 2 vols. Reprint, New York: Greenwood Press, 1968.

Leo Oppenheim, ed., *Letters from Mesopotamia: Official, Business, and Private Letters on Clay Tablets from Two Millennia*. Chicago: University of Chicago Press, 1967.

Plutarch, *Life of Alexander*, in *Plutarch: The Age of Alexander*. Trans. Ian Scott-Kilvert. New York: Penguin Books, 1973.

James B. Pritchard, ed., *Ancient Near Eastern Texts Relating to the Old Testament*. Princeton: Princeton University Press, 1969.

Martha T. Roth, *Law Collections from Mesopotamia and Asia Minor*. Atlanta: Scholars Press, 1995.

George Smith, *Assyrian Discoveries*. New York: Scribner, 1875.

Leroy Waterman, ed., *Royal Correspondence of the Assyrian Empire*. 4 vols. Ann Arbor: University of Michigan Press, 1930-1936.

Xenophon, *Anabasis*, published as *The March Up Country*. Trans. W.H.D. Rouse. New York: New American Library, 1959.

———, *Cyropaedia*. Trans. Walter Miller, 2 vols. New York: Macmillan, 1914.

———, *Hellenica*, published as *A History of My Times*. Trans. Rex Warner. New York: Penguin Books, 1979.

Additional Works Consulted

Paul G. Bahn, ed., *The Cambridge Illustrated History of Archaeology.* New York: Cambridge University Press, 1996.

Alessandro Bausani, *The Persians: From the Earliest Days to the Twentieth Century.* Trans. J.B. Donne. London: Elek, 1971.

Jean Bottero, *Mesopotamia: Writing, Reasoning, and the Gods.* Trans. Zainab Bahrani and Marc Van De Mieroop. Chicago: University of Chicago Press, 1992.

————, *Religion in Ancient Mesopotamia.* Trans. Teresa L. Fagan. Chicago: University of Chicago Press, 2001.

James Henry Breasted, *A Brief History of Ancient Times.* Long Beach, CA: Lost Arts Media, 2003. Reprint of Breasted's classic *Ancient Times: A History of the Early World.*

Trevor Bryce, *The Kingdom of the Hittites.* Oxford: Clarendon Press, 1998.

L. Sprague de Camp, *The Ancient Engineers.* New York: Ballantine, 1963.

C.W. Ceram, *Gods, Graves, and Scholars: The Story of Archaeology.* Trans. E.B. Garside and Sophie Wilkins. New York: Random House, 1986.

Peter Clayton and Martin Price, *The Seven Wonders of the Ancient World.* New York: Barnes and Noble, 1993.

Georges Contenau, *Everyday Life in Babylon and Assyria.* London: Edward Arnold, 1964.

J.M. Cook, *The Persian Empire.* London: Dent, 1983.

L. Delaporte, *Mesopotamia: The Babylonian and Assyrian Civilization.* Trans. V. Gordon Childe. New York: Barnes and Noble, 1970.

Willam G. Dever, *Who Were the Early Israelites and Where Did They Come From?* Grand Rapids, MI: William B. Eerdman's, 2003.

Robert Drews, *The Coming of the Greeks: Indo-European Conquests in the Aegean and the Near East.* Princeton: Princeton University Press, 1988.

————, *The End of the Bronze Age: Changes in Warfare and the Catastrophe ca. 1200 B.C.* Princeton: Princeton University Press, 1993.

Henri Frankfort, *Art and Architecture of the Ancient Orient.* New York: Penguin, 1971.

Ilya Gershevitch, ed., *The Cambridge History of Iran.* Volume 2: *The Median and Achaemenian Periods.* Cambridge, UK: Cambridge University Press, 1985.

Michael Grant, *The Ancient Mediterranean.* New York: Penguin, 1969.

———, *The Visible Past.* New York: Scribner's, 1990.

A. Kirk Grayson, *Assyrian Rulers of the Third and Second Millennia B.C.* Toronto: University of Toronto Press, 1987.

Sir John Hackett, ed., *Warfare in the Ancient World.* New York: Facts On File, 1989.

Roberta L. Harris, *The World of the Bible.* London: Thames and Hudson, 1995.

Tom B. Jones, ed., *The Sumerian Problem.* New York: John Wiley, 1969.

Samuel N. Kramer, *History Begins at Sumer.* Philadelphia: University of Pennsylvania Press, 1981.

———, *Sumerian Mythology.* New York: Harper and Row, 1972.

Seton Lloyd, *The Archaeology of Mesopotamia.* London: Thames and Hudson, 1978.

———, *Foundations in the Dust: A Story of Mesopotamian Exploration.* New York: Thames and Hudson, 1981.

———, *The Ruined Cities of Iraq.* Chicago: Ares, 1980.

James Mellaart, *Earliest Civilizations of the Near East.* New York: McGraw-Hill, 1965.

P.R.S. Moorey, *Ancient Mesopotamian Materials and Industries.* Oxford: Oxford University Press, 1994.

———, *A Century of Biblical Archaeology.* Cambridge, UK: Cambridge University Press, 1991.

Joan Oates, *Babylon.* London: Thames and Hudson, 1986.

A.T. Olmstead, *History of Assyria.* 1923. Reprint, Chicago: University of Chicago Press, 1968.

Andre Parrot, *The Arts of Assyria.* New York: Golden Press, 1961.

———, *Sumer: The Dawn of Art.* Golden Press, 1961.

Nicholas Postgate and J.N. Postgate, *Early Mesopotamia: Society and Economy at the Dawn of History.* New York: Routledge, 1994.

Julian Reade, *Mesopotamia.* Cambridge, MA: Harvard University Press, 1991.

John M. Russell, *Sennacherib's Palace Without Rival at Nineveh.* Chicago: University of Chicago Press, 1991.

William Ryan and Walter Pitman, *Noah's Flood: The New Scientific Discoveries About the Event That Changed History.* New York: Simon and Schuster, 1998.

H.W.F. Saggs, *The Greatness That Was Babylon.* New York: New American Library, 1963.

———, *The Might That Was Assyria.* London: Sidgwick and Jackson, 1984.

J.M. Sasson, ed., *Civilizations of the Near East.* 4 vols. New York: Scribner's, 1995.

Wolfram von Soden, *The Ancient Orient: An Introduction to the Study of the Ancient Near East.* Trans. Donald G. Schley. Grand Rapids, MI: William B. Eerdmans, 1994.

Chester G. Starr, *A History of the Ancient World*. New York: Oxford University Press, 1991.

Sir Percy Sykes, *A History of Persia*. 1915. 2 vols. Reprint, London: Macmillan, 1958.

Michael Wood, *Legacy: The Search for Ancient Cultures*. New York: Sterling, 1992.

Charles Leonard Woolley, *Digging Up the Past*. Baltimore: Penguin, 1937.

————, *The Sumerians*. New York: Norton, 1965.

————, *Ur Excavations*. 8 vols. London: British Museum, 1934–1982.

Index

artistic depiction of events in, 48
Hammurabi and, 32
independence of, 67
ruins of, 86
sacking of, by Babylon and Media, 69
Nippur (Sumeria), 18
Noah. *See* Atrahasis

Old Babylonian Period, 28
Old Testament
city of Erech in, 17
great flood of, 14
2 Chronicles, 47–48
oracle at Delphi, 74
Ottoman Turks, 93

Palestine
Alexander the Great and, 86
Assyrian Empire and, 43–44, 47
Cyrus and, 74
Egypt and, 37
Fertile Crescent and, 10
Muslim conquest of, 93
Psamtik and, 51
Parthian Empire, 91–92
Pasargadae, 71–72
Pelusium (Egypt), 75
People of Ancient Assyria: Their Inscriptions and Correspondence (Laessoe), 30
Persepolis (Persia), 80
Persian Empire, 10, 68, 93
foreign competition with, 74
largest empire, 75
Mesopotamian culture and, 53
Persian Gulf, 10, 17

Assyrian Empire and, 43, 51
geography of, 14
road to, 77
Sargon at, 19
Sumerians and, 15
Persians, The (Vellacott), 83
Phraortes, 70
Philip II, 86
Phrygia, 78
Pitman, Walter, 13–14
Plataea, 83
Plutarch, 86–87
politics
city-states and, 15
fragmentation of, 40
kingship and, 18
unification and, 19
Psammetichos III (Psamtik), 51, 75
Ptolemy, 88

Qabra, 30

religion
Assyrian crusades and, 40–41
land ownership and, 55–56
Sumerian, 27
ziggurat and, 18
Rimush, 20
Romans, 91–92
Ryan, William, 13–14

Saka people, 78
Salamis (Greece), 82–83
Samsu-ditana, 34
Samsu-iluna, 33
Sardis (Lydia)
Cyrus and, 74
Darius and, 80
roads to, 77–78

Sargon of Akkad, 16, 18–20, 91
Sargon II, 26
conquest of Urartu by, 44
treaty with Medes by, 67
wall sculpture and, 48
Sāsānians Empire, 92
Scythia, 78–80
Seleucia on the Tigris, 89–90
Seleucus, 93
Babylon and, 89
civil strife and, 91
Hellenistic culture, 88
social structure of, 90
Sennacherib, 44, 46
assassination of, 49
on drawing water from wells, 62
"Palace Without Rival" and, 48
Palestine and, 47–48
Shalmaneser I, 39
Shalmaneser III, 43
Shamash (deity), 31
Shamash-shum-ukin, 52
Shamshi-Adad, 29–31
Shamshi-Adad V, 43
Shulgi, 23
Shunham, 30
Sidon (Palestine), 47, 50
Sin (deity), 54
Sin-shar-ishkun, 66
Skudra, 80
Smith, George, 25
social structure
in Fertile Crescent, 13
Greek, 90
laborers in, 57
legal rights of slaves, 58
nobles and priests, 55–56
under Parthians, 92
tradition-based, 53

Picture Credits

Cover: Mary Evans Picture Library

© Yann Arthus-Bertrand/CORBIS, 12

© Bettmann/CORBIS, 54

© Werner Forman/Art Resource, NY, 57

© Chris Hellier/CORBIS, 13

Hulton Archive/Getty Images, 85

© David Lees/CORBIS, 94

© Erich Lessing/Art Resource, NY, 21, 26, 43, 46, 47, 59, 61, 63, 68, 91

Library of Congress, 86

North Wind Picture Archives, 85

© Gianni Dagli Orti/CORBIS, 56

© Reunion des Musees Nationaux/Art Resource, NY, 35

© Scala/Art Resource, NY, 19, 36

© SEF/Art Resource, NY, 71, 80

Jane Sweeney/Lonely Planet Images, 17

© Nik Wheeler/CORBIS, 29

© Roger Wood/CORBIS, 93

© Michael S. Yamashita/CORBIS, 22

About the Author

Historian and award-winning writer Don Nardo has published many books about the ancient world, including *Life in Ancient Athens, Life of a Roman Gladiator, Egyptian Mythology*, literary companions to the works of Homer, Sophocles, and Euripides, histories of the Assyrian and Persian Empires, and the *Greenhaven Encyclopedia of Greek and Roman Mythology*. He lives with his wife, Christine, in Massachusetts.